ACT JUSTLY

OR 15 drama sketches to solve the world's problems

ACT JUSTLY

or 15 drama sketches to solve the world's problems

Christian Aid

THE CHURCHES IN ACTION WITH THE WORLD'S POOR

1962-1987

CAFOD JUBILEE

On the side of people in need

COLLINS

Collins Liturgical Publications
8 Grafton Street, London W1X 3LA

Distributed in Ireland by
Educational Company of Ireland
21 Talbot Street, Dublin 1

Collins Liturgical Australia
PO Box 316, Blackburn, Victoria 3130

ISBN 0 00 599958 8
© 1987 CAFOD and Christian Aid
First published 1987

Performing rights

Typographical design by Colin Reed
Typeset by John Swain Limited, Glasgow
Made and printed by William Collins Sons & Co Ltd, Glasgow

CONTENTS

Curtain Raisers: duration under 3 minutes

Act 1: duration 3-6 minutes

Contents

Act 2: duration 7-14 minutes

Act 3: duration 15-20 minutes

PREFACE

Christian Aid and the Catholic Fund for Overseas Development (CAFOD) would like to express sincere thanks to the many people who have helped to make this book possible.

In particular we would like to thank: Jim Belben of the Bible Society and the Revd Mark Davies of Revelation Ministries for their invaluable advice on the Editorial Group and the Revd Chris Wright of the Union Biblical Seminary, Pune, India, for extensive help with the Bible notes; John Cleese and Graham Chapman for permission to print *The Tea Shop* which is based on an original idea by them; Sheila Fairbairn and Alan Foss and all those whose work we have read, even if it is not included in the book.

Kevin Yell   Martin Leach
CAFOD   Christian Aid

FOREWORD

When Jesus Christ spoke to his followers in parables, it was not to disguise the truth but rather to help them to understand a difficult theme by starting from a like situation easily within their experience.

For those living in the relative security and affluence of the West, it is not always easy to understand the degree of poverty and deprivation of opportunity which development organizations seek to relieve. Statistics soon reach saturation point. Even the starvation photographs used in appeals gradually lose novelty and impact.

On the other hand, drama is fast becoming recognized as a powerful means of communication and education in the Church. There is increasing demand for material and scripts of professional quality, suitable for use in schools, parishes, youth clubs and Third World Groups.

This development drama book has been prepared with this in mind. The concern of CAFOD and Christian Aid is with social justice and morality, with economic development and the relief of hunger, with the equitable use of the rich resources entrusted to humankind by God. It also has to deal with the sinfulness of the greed which conditions relief to self-interest, and the immorality of the exploitation of the powerless masses by the few.

It is easy to shut out such thoughts as political propaganda, especially when they relate to events beyond our personal experience. The argument that 'we have enough troubles of our own' does not acquit us of the responsibilities to our distant neighbours whose human rights and dignity are denied.

We hope that these plays and sketches will help to bring home this point, to break through the barrier of non-comprehension owing to inexperience. The study pages accompanying the scripts show the Biblical foundation for what is portrayed by drama. We see the relevance today of the great themes of Genesis and Ecclesiastes about the generous abundance provided by the Creator and the dangers when possessions are misused.

This book should fill a need which is known to exist. We trust it will itself bring help and hope to the real people who lie behind the statistics of the experts and the living parables here presented.

+DEREK WORLOCK
Archbishop of Liverpool

+DAVID SHEPPARD
Bishop of Liverpool

An ancient motorbike wheezed into a village square in Eastern India. Squashed between the local bank manager at the front and the doctor on the back was a tired and travel-weary young Englishman. Peering at his notebook he asked himself 'What now? Community organization, supplementary feeding or well digging? Ah — Wednesday— it's drama by the youth group.'

The women and young children were sitting expectantly on the ground in front of a makeshift open air platform. The men were rushing round trying to fix the loudspeakers which kept fusing the lighting. When all was ready and the dignitaries had made their speeches, the event that everyone had really come for started — the play.

It was nothing fancy, no laser lights or complicated sets, just simple dialogue on a plain board stage. But it was effective.

At the end of the night the men had learnt that they had legal rights against eviction by the landlord, and the women saw the need for group training in health care.

Nellutan village had moved further on the road to self-development, not through the advice of technical experts, but with the help of a twenty minute sketch.

That drama gave the young Englishman an idea. If development drama can mobilize an Indian village, then surely it can do the same for churches in the West. This book is born out of that idea. . . .

The scripts

This book is for drama groups with an interest in development and development groups who want to try drama. There is a script here for everyone, whether you belong to an experienced theatre company or to a Third World study group.

The sketches deliberately vary in length, style and depth of analysis of the subject. For example, Alan MacDonald's *Political Prisoners* is a considered treatment of the dilemmas facing Christians in violent situations, helpful for reflective discussion, whilst Simon Parke's *Charity begins at* is quick and punchy, useful as a sermon illustration.

Therefore, before selecting a script for performance you should ask yourself a number of questions about how you intend to use the piece. What is the occasion at which the sketch will be performed? Is it street theatre, a church service or a special gathering? Who are the audience, and what is their level of understanding of world poverty and development? What message do you want to communicate? Would more information on the subject be helpful? How much time will you have to perform, and will there be a chance to discuss the sketch with the audience? The answers to questions like these will help you to select which of the sketches is most appropriate for your needs.

The Workshop by Jim Belben is a simple lead-in session. You will find it useful if you want to increase your understanding of development or to brush up your acting skills. It is a straightforward one and a half hour programme with a number of warm-up games, role plays and improvisations. Teaching dramatic technique or development theory is not the purpose of this book of sketches, but a number of helpful titles do exist for this and they can be found in the book list on page 126.

The Bible notes

'All this stuff about development is very exciting, even fashionable, but what has it to do with Christianity?' Is social justice really something that God's people should be involved in? Is it a priority for a Christian's time?

These are questions that anyone using this book is likely to be asked, and ones that Christian Aid and CAFOD regularly have to face. The Bible notes found with each sketch in Acts 1, 2 and 3 will help provide some answers.

Compiled from specially commissioned work by the Revd Chris Wright, the notes give an overview of how the Bible treats each topic and show how issues of poverty and economic security are of central importance to God's relationship with humanity, past, present and future.

This approach is designed to help groups gain understanding of the Biblical background to the topic on which they are working. The references included give directions for Bible study.

The follow up

'Suppose a brother or sister is without clothes and daily food. If one of you says to him, "Go, I wish you well; keep warm and well fed," but does nothing about his physical needs, what good is it?' (James 2:15-16, *NIV*). In other words, 'Don't just stand there, do something!'

This book is designed to help Christians consider the questions of world poverty and development and then to make a suitably active response.

To equip you to do this each follow up is divided into two parts. The first has three questions which are useful as a sermon guide, or for small group discussion of the sketch and its application. The second part has three action ideas. But be careful! Select your activity sensitively. Make sure you suggest activities appropriate to the level of understanding of your audience. Suggesting highly committed action after a first performance of a one minute sketch could undo all the positive work you are trying to achieve!

Some ideas apply to more than one sketch. Also, you may think of others for yourself. If you need any assistance do not hesitate to contact the appropriate agency, addresses on pages 124-5.

We have enjoyed bringing this book together and are sure it will be a great resource for development education and fund raising. We hope you enjoy performing the sketches and using them to fulfil the words of scripture:

> This is what Yahweh asks of you:
> only this, to act justly,
> to love tenderly
> and to walk humbly with your God.
> (Micah 6:8, *JB*)

Kevin Yell   Martin Leach
CAFOD   Christian Aid

A preparatory workshop can make the difference between a flabby final performance and a tight one. It can also make the difference between communicating your message and missing the point entirely.

The aim of a development drama workshop is to help you to experience some basic development issues before you start trying to communicate them. 'Obvious', you may think, but it's surprising how many people make the mistake of thinking a drama group can perform a sketch without understanding what lies behind it.

What's more, having fun together — and drama workshops are more about fun than anything else — can make your acting so much better.

How to plan a workshop

First you must have a leader. If you turn up hoping that someone will have some bright ideas on the night, you'll be disappointed. Appoint a person who isn't rushed off their feet with other commitments, someone who can put some thought into planning the workshop.

Find a room that is big enough for your group to move around in freely — and if it's got a carpet, all the better. If you are going to use music make sure there is a power point and remember to bring, beg or borrow a powerful cassette player.

The workshop should last at least ninety minutes. Two hours is ideal. And do warn people beforehand to wear loose comfortable clothes. Some drama games can be quite embarrassing if you're wearing the latest high street fashions!

The aim of the workshop is to relax people and allow them to explore their dramatic abilities. Granted, the workshop does have a serious point but don't let that fool you into planning some really heavy and tragic improvisations. If at the end people can say 'I really enjoyed that', and 'I never realized how easy it is to make up a character', count it as a success.

A typical workshop should consist of

⋆Ice breakers	approx. 10 minutes
⋆Physical warm up	approx. 10 minutes
⋆Improvisation singly and in pairs	approx. 25 minutes
⋆Improvisation in groups	approx. 20 minutes
⋆Closing activity	approx. 10 minutes

Observant readers will note that this doesn't add up to ninety minutes, but things always overrun, and you have to allow time between activities for people to discuss what they have just done. However, one other golden rule is to plan more activities than you think you will need, because if something does finish early it always seems impossible to think of ideas on the spot. So plan ahead. And overplan.

It's not too fanciful to compare a workshop to a wave — particularly as it appears to a surfer. First, you've got to get out to the wave. In a workshop the warm-ups and early exercises help you to do this. Then you get up on your board and ride the wave of dramatic inspiration for a while. Then you drop off. But don't leave the surfer out there or you'll have a drowned duck on your hands. To get back to shore you need some sort of closing activity.

Jim Belben

It belongs to me

by Jim Belben

Objective

To look at ownership and possessions and see how they may relate to the wider development issue of resources and their unfair allocation and use.

Undoubtedly the best workshop is the one you design yourself with your own group in mind. So although you can use this workshop as it stands, it is much better to use it as a structure on which you can hang your own ideas.

It will show you how you can combine games and drama exercises to explore an issue. It will also show you the purpose behind each phase of a workshop.

The warm up

Lack of concentration and lack of trust can be as much of a problem as a 'cold' body, so it is important that your warm up includes both games to get people working well with others, and physical exercises to get them working well with their own bodies!

Ice breakers

Use any games that you know. But if you're stuck for where to start here are two examples.

Buster

Collect four balls of various sizes. For example, a marble, a golf ball, a tennis ball and a football.

Everyone sits in a circle, feet into the circle. Put the biggest ball in the middle. The objective is to kick the ball out of the circle. Easy? The catch is you have to stay sitting and you can only kick it with the soles of your feet.

After a while, change to the next smallest ball, and so on down to the marble.

If they still want more put all four balls in together.

And don't ask me why it's called Buster. I don't know either!

5 minutes

Log rolling

The group play the logs, not the Canadian lumberjacks.

Everyone lies down on the floor. (You can ask them to lie in a row if you want a more organized version of this game.) Then with eyes closed they roll about randomly — and over one another, if someone happens to be in the way. Watch out for vicious knees and elbows. The point of this exercise is to get people to relax — even when they're in close physical contact with someone else.

Not to be played after a big meal!

5 minutes

Physical warm up

A physical warm up gets your body ready for action.

If you're looking for ideas Gordon and Ronni Lamont's *Move Yourselves* offers many useful tips for working on cold cholesterol-infested bodies. (See Booklist.) Here are two examples of physical warm ups.

Grunters

Everyone stands with their feet eighteen inches apart. They then flop forwards — not a stretching movement but a relaxed, flopping movement — and let their arms dangle.

Repeat but this time let out a sigh as you collapse and breathe in as you slowly rise up again. Repeat to left and right.

After a couple of goes, change the noise first to a squeal and then to a deep groan or grunt.

If people only make timid weak sounds to start with, coax them into a bold liberating noise by the example you set as you illustrate the exercise.

5 minutes

Spacewalk

If you can lay on zero gravity for the workshop skip this activity. But assuming you're rehearsing in some church hall very much this side of the ozone layer, a spacewalk can help get those muscles working.

Put on some disco music with a strong beat. Everyone walks around in time with the music. When you're sure people have picked up the beat, get them counting with you in Jane Fonda-Aerobics style, 1,2,3,4,5,6, sev-en, 8 (emphasis falls on 7), and walking in time as they count.

Now on a specified step everyone must make that step into a giant moonsized leap. Start by leaping on sev-en. That's the easiest.

Follow that with leaping on even numbers, stepping on the rest. Then leap on odd numbers, step the rest.

Then try some random numbers shouted by the leader or the participants.

Finally, leap on all numbers. The results, probably with one or two notable pot-bellied exceptions, might look a little like ballet. Shatter the illusion of brilliance by repeating the same exercise but walking backwards! Repeat again walking sideways.

5 minutes

Improvization singly and in pairs

Improvization in this context means simply making up a scene. The best way to do it is to build up in stages. First you are on your own. Then you make up a scene with someone else. Then do it as a whole group.

On your own
Find a space to yourself.

Choose an object in the room. Anything at all. Take that object back to your space. Investigate uses for that object. As many as possible and as unusual or imaginative as possible. A chair could be a grandfather clock, a step-ladder, a houseplant.

Choose one favourite use. From now on that is what your possession is. You should behave appropriately. For example, if your handbag is a sack of coal — you should pull it around as if it was heavy and dirty.

3-5 minutes

Now develop a character to go with your possession. If your sweater is an oriental rug then you might be a rug salesman, or a rich woman who's just bought it. You might be a refuse collector who has just picked it up from a skip. You might be a child who believes this is a magic carpet etc. The possibilities are endless.

2-3 minutes

Now start moving around the room, in character, with your object. If you are an old lady with a deep freeze — alias a hymn book — you may not make much progress. But if you are a policeman who has just discovered the stolen diamond necklace of the Countess of Ping Pong masquerading as a coffee cup, you'll be anxious to get it back to the owner intact.

2 minutes

Pairs
When the leader gives the signal, you start to interact with others. You meet another character and, still in role, explain to them the qualities of your possession, what you are doing with it, and what your plans are for it.

2 minutes

N.B. After this first interaction some people may want to change or improve their object or their character; this is allowed.

Move on and repeat, meeting another character. 2 minutes

Finally, repeat a third time. This time your meeting has a new objective. You must try to convince the other character that your possession is more valuable to you than theirs is — for whatever reason.

3 minutes

Leader Draw everyone together. Get each person to explain very briefly who they are and what object they are carrying around with them. Draw out how they feel about their valued possession.

Improvization in groups

Groups (1)
Join with two other people.

Now the moment of parting arrives. Two of your possessions must be laid aside so that as a group you can concentrate on just one of the three objects. Choose together whose it will be. It should be the most 'valued' object!

3 minutes

Create a scene, shorter than two minutes, in which the possession is somehow mislaid, lost, stolen, hijacked or burned, decays or explodes, and, if you wish, is recovered.

5-7 minutes

You can keep the same characters as earlier, or invent new ones.

Leader Watch each short scene. As you do, investigate the feeling that lies behind the ownership of possessions.

7-10 minutes

Link
The final part of the workshop involves a change of pace, and a broadening of the subject. So now play a game that gives you a clean break. How about 'knee slap'? Choose a partner who has roughly the same shoe size as you. You must try to slap their knees. The first to give five slaps is the winner.

Repeat if you wish, as a knockout contest, ending up with a 'knee slap' final.

2-5 minutes

Groups (2)
Many groups feel dissatisfied if they have nothing to 'show' for an improvization. So the aim of this last period is to create a more consciously 'performable' sketch. Though the likelihood of it being performable as it stands is very small indeed!

You will need to make some link such as: 'So far we have been looking at our feelings, and our characters' feelings about possessions . . . (summarize some of the earlier findings). Did you know that the word 'private' comes from the same word as 'deprive'? If we own something we are depriving someone else of it. The final bit of our workshop looks at this.'

Get into groups, preferably the same as in groups (1).

Create a one minute sketch called *It Belongs to Me,* as unsubtle as you like — in fact the more obvious the better — in which the message is to show how someone's ownership of an item deprives somebody else of that item. It can be tragic, comical, poetic, lyrical, epic, mythical. It could be in the form of pantomime, or a musical sketch. You could use simply mime and no words. You could add sound effects to give it more zip.

Leader If the group needs some more help suggest a model for them, for example, *Before and After:* one scene showing a situation when someone was keeping a possession to themselves, a second showing what the situation was when they shared it.

Get together and watch the sketches.

Leader Get people to pick out what they feel are the strong points of each sketch — remember, people need all the encouragement they can get!

10 minutes

Closing activity

Sharing the biscuit

After drawing together any final comments from the group, finish with this 'meditation activity', which is a picture of how we can share our resources with others.

Most of the people using this book will be part of the rich world which, with only one quarter of the people, consumes more than two thirds of the food, even more of the energy, and despite all our pretensions to generosity, we in the developed world are extracting more in debt repayments than we are giving out in aid.

As a symbol of our wish to share our resources more equally, think through any part of your life in which you could share more of what you have — it doesn't have to be money; it could be time, talents or whatever — and then tell one other person of what you think you could share more.

4-5 minutes

Then to symbolize this, pass round a digestive biscuit. Each person takes a piece of biscuit as it comes around.

2 minutes

Curtain Raisers

duration under 3 minutes

Introduction

If you have ever needed a quick piece of drama as a starter to a sermon or as a comment before a group discussion then you will find these 'Curtain Raisers' very useful.

Charity Begins At   A thirty second duologue leading into anything to do with fund raising.

The Holy Words   For those who remember the Peter Cook-Dudley Moore sketches, here is one in that style, looking at the youth of today and their attitude to the 'Holy Words of Jesus'.

The Blame   Of a similar style to *The Holy Words,* this longer piece looks at apportioning the blame for the state of the world today.

Dives   A short and challenging adaptation of the Dives and Lazarus story.

Project Report   This poem is a good piece to focus thoughts on attitudes to giving and as an introduction to the concept that the relationship between 'donors' and 'recipients' is often reversed.

Charity Begins At

by Simon Parke

(B *Shakes Tin. Enter* A.)

A: What are you collecting for?

B: Quids for Kids.

A: Quids for Kids. Good cause that. After all, they are the next generation.

B: Right. And I mean if we don't care, who will?

A: Yeh — I can see well enough why you give up your Saturdays to collect money.

B: Yeh — (*Pause*) — mind you, it's not the only reason I do it.

A: Oh? Well, what's the other?

B: Can't stand having the kids around the house at weekends.

The Holy Words

by Simon Parke

(*Two disgruntled men stand and talk.*)

T: The trouble with the youth of today, George — they just don't have time for the holy words of Jesus.

G: Very true, Trev.

T: They'll help the poor, mind.

G: Oh yes, they'll help the poor.

T: And they'll speak out for the captives, all right.

T: *And* work to rid the world of blindness.

G: Yes, that as well.

T: *And* fight for the oppressed of the world, of course.

G: Don't need to tell me, Trev — they'll fight for the oppressed all hours of the day, it seems.

T: And yet, do you know what they don't have time for, George?

G: What's that, Trev?

T: They don't have time for the holy words of Jesus. Makes you weep, doesn't it?

The Blame

by Simon Parke

(*The two Mels stand side by side.*)

MEL 1: Know what, Mel?

MEL 2: What's that, Mel?

MEL 1: It's a mess, Mel.

MEL 2: What's a mess, Mel?

MEL 1: This country, Mel.

MEL 2: Oh yeah — this country's a mess, and no mistake.

MEL 1: Very true.

MEL 2: That we can say.

MEL 1: Yep.

MEL 2: With no dispute.

MEL 1: Nope.

MEL 2: This country is a mess.

MEL 1: Right.

MEL 2: Right.

MEL 1: Right. So . . . er . . .

MEL 2: So what?

MEL 1: So who can we blame?

MEL 2: How d'you mean?

MEL 1: Who can we blame?

MEL 2: Blame?

MEL 1: Blame! For the mess!

MEL 2: Oh yeah — the mess.

MEL 1: We've got to blame someone.

MEL 2: True.

MEL 1: Cos I'm not taking the blame.

MEL 2: Oh.

MEL 1: Well are you taking the blame?

MEL 2: Oh no Mel — I'm not taking the blame.

MEL 1: No — I didn't think so. So who is?

MEL 2: Who is what?

MEL 1: Taking the blame!

MEL 2: Oh yeah — taking the blame. (*Pause*) Well, I don't know — we could ask Gary if he would.

MEL 1: Gary's a friend.

MEL 2: Well how about your dad?

MEL 1: You can't ask *family*.

MEL 2: Bit difficult then cos if you can't choose friends or family, that just leaves all those we *don't* know — you know, people who are different from us. And I mean, we can hardly blame them, can we?

MEL 1: Why not?

MEL 2: (*Pause*) Well —

MEL 1: They sound pretty ideal to me —

MEL 2: (*Pause*) But . . .

MEL 1: I mean, we blame them cos they *are* different.

MEL 2: Do you think so?

MEL 1: Well, why should they be different? What's wrong with us and the way *we* do things?

MEL 2: Nothing at all.

MEL 1: Think they know it all, do they?

MEL 2: Think they know better than us?

MEL 1: They look different.

MEL 2: Dress different.

MEL 1: Cook different.

MEL 2: Think different.

MEL 1: Act different — I mean, what's their game? No wonder this country's in a mess! Do you know who I blame?

MEL 2: Who?

MEL 1: Every one who's different!

(*The following section involves increasing pace, frenzied pointing and a crescendo of noise.*)

MEL 2: I blame *them* — and *them* — and *them* —

MEL 1: And *them* — and *them* — and *them* —

M AND M: (*Alternately, then merging*) And *them* — and *them* — and *them* — and *them* — and *them* (*etc. etc.*) (*Stillness*)

MEL 1: Makes you feel better, doesn't it?

MEL 2: What?

MEL 1: Passing the blame.

Dives

by Simon Parke

x: I'd like to tell you a story. I'm sure it couldn't happen today of course. But it's a sad story nevertheless. And it's about this man called Dives. And he was rich, all right?

(*Enter A on other side of stage, oblivious to x as x is to A. Throughout, A shouts to figure off stage — probably 'upstairs'.*)

A: I'm home darling!

x: And he lived a comfortable life.

A: Shall I pour you a sherry?

x: And basically he was a good man I suppose.

A: I've put two pounds into the collection* envelope. (**Name envelope as appropriate.*)

x: Not a great saint, no — but not a great sinner either.

A: Yes, I know it's the same as we gave last year, darling, but we do have to be sensible with our money.

x: Like I said, a good man —

A: We'll give more next year maybe —

x: Society would call him good anyway —

A: After all, we can't solve the world's problems by ourselves!

x: Mainly, of course, because he never did anything that was very obviously wrong.

A: Oh and by the way, I'm playing golf tomorrow with this accountant chappie who says he might be able to do us a few financial favours.

x: And he was a religious man, our Dives.

A: Met him in church would you believe? Who knows — it could be the Canaries for us this year instead of next, if he comes up trumps.

x: Clean living and decent would have been his *own* estimation of himself.

A: Seems like Rob and Jenny have gone their separate ways — can't imagine how she stuck him so long.

x: Yet Dives, when he died — and this pulled me up a bit I can tell you — when he died, he went to hell.

a: Your sherry's ready!

x: Not because he *did* anything —

a: And so am I!

x: No, Dives went to hell because he *didn't* do anything. Could never happen today of course. (*Exits*)

a: I got the film I wanted. Thought we could watch it tonight — together.

(*For the first time, casts shifty eye over to where x had been standing. And then back to his business. Slightly strained —*)

a: Yes, I feel like a good film tonight . . .

Project Report

by John Coutts

A dramatic poem

(*A missionary working in Lagos, Nigeria, received a grant to provide Christmas cheer for old people. He helped to share the gifts and received an unexpected blessing. He is recording on tape a report explaining how the grant was spent.*)

SPEAKER: 'To Projects Officer, P.O. Box, etcetera:

Dear Sir,
     The grant you gave was used as follows:
We purchased thirty plastic bags. In each
We placed a pound of rice, some tea, dried beans,
St Matthew's gospel in the local language,
Sugar and salt, a box of matches, tinned
Tomato puree, local leaves resembling
Spinach, bananas, oranges, some palm
Oil, and a greeting card'

                      New paragraph.

     'The funds, we trust were wisely spent; the list
Of aged people checked and double-checked
In case of fraud. The bags were packed on Christmas
Eve, and taken round by volunteers
On Christmas Day. Each team included one
At least who spoke the local language. I
Myself took part . . .'

(*The speaker stops dictating and starts remembering.*)

     Old woman, please forgive.
We came to help. I never knew your home
Was bare, so very bare; the walls unpainted

Concrete: never thought we'd scare you stiff,
We strangers bearing gifts. You saw and dreaded
My whitish face and khaki shorts, my thin
Thin lips and pointed nose. Was it police?
Or Taxmen? Trouble — yes, official trouble!
We gave you such a fright on Christmas morning
Attempting to deliver one of thirty
Plastic bags containing . . . never mind . . .
For once you understood, you offered thanks
In long melodious words and solemn gestures
Centuries old. You greeted Khaki Shorts
(Who hardly knows the local language) kindly,
Maternally, a queen beside your charcoal
Fire: then you smiled and made your farewell curtsey
Slowly and gently, being old, but smoothly,
As though the years had spared your maidenhood.
You blessed me then. We went our way unsnubbed
And you unpatronized.

                                        Let's try again.

(*And so back to the dictation*)

'To Projects Officer, P.O. Box, etcetera:

   Dear Sir,
         The grant you gave was used as follows . . .'

Act 1

duration 3-6 minutes

What's Yours is Mine

by Simon Parke after Chief Seattle

The more precious you feel a gift is, the greater care you take of it. The Bible presents the whole of the created order as God's magnificent gift to the human race. God's intention was clearly that humans should care for and utilize the rich resources entrusted to them.

Likewise the Psalms celebrate not only God's delight in creation, but also its availability for human cultivation and enjoyment.

However, different people value these gifts in very different ways. Are they assets for us to use and dominate, or are they gifts of which we are the stewards?

Characters   A represents Business
B represents The People
C Narrator

Stage Directions
The sketch's simple format and lack of props make it widely usable. All three characters speak facing straight forward, seemingly ignoring each other. It may be suitable to dress A in a suit and B in casual clothes. C stands in between them but slightly back.

C: I had a dream — and in my dream I saw two men stand in a dock. One stood powerful and confident, and I remember he smiled a lot. He had a winning way, that one. The other man was different, slightly stooped. He didn't smile. And it was odd — but I sensed in that courtroom that he wasn't liked . . .

A: The bulldozers moved in in early morning, you understand, in order to avoid any trouble. We do try to avoid it, of course. Not that the land wasn't ours —

B: 'Mine' 'Yours' 'Ours' — the day such labels were invented was the beginning of the end.

A: Three years of courtcases had seen to that, but you've got to hand it to these Indians — they're fighters! A law unto themselves!

B: It is not a troublesome thing to uphold the law, when it is part of your syndicate.

A: You wouldn't believe there were people like that still around!

B: There won't be for long.

A: But there are, there really are! Alive and well in the 1980's and kicking up all sorts of trouble! You tell them about technology, you tell them — and it's as if they don't hear!

B: We never heard what they said, because we saw too clearly what they were.

A: I mean, let me say right away, we have bent over backwards —

B: The court case took longer than expected —

A: Believe me, we have listened and listened and listened —

B: And still failed to understand —

A: We came to them as friends!

B: They came as thieves in the night, to snatch from the land.

A: I mean, no one loves open spaces more than I, no one! But let's keep things in perspective — God's earth is there to be conquered!

B: Honoured —

A: And we are experienced in land —

B: They've done it before —

A: Helpers!

B: Strangers. The earth is no brother of theirs. It is an enemy, a subversive, to be bought, tamed, conquered, squeezed, dealt in, dirtied, sold, left and forgotten —

A: Our work, of course, is primarily for future generations —

B: They kidnap the world from their children and shout 'Progress' as cover —

A: Progress! And proud of it! We're going to put this wasteland to work!

B: They'll put this homeland to death. They found a garden — they'll leave a desert. They always do. They'll talk of civilization —

A: Civilization!

B: And only at the end, only at the very end — will they mention —

A: Profit, yes. Let us not pretend for one moment that there is no financial benefit in this for us. Of course there is! We can't run a charity!

B: Despots need finance —

A: We're a business!

B: They're a conspiracy —

A: (*Gentler — compassionate*) Yes, there will be problems afterwards, there always are of course, and it's very, very regret-
table. But then, you see, we merely set the project up. What
happens afterwards to the land and people — they're not,
frankly, our responsibility —

B: Rest assured, they will be no one's —

A: Other agencies must continue the work —

B: You know, it only struck me as I saw the machines start work
and the buildings go up; as I heard the cars start and the music
whine — it struck me only then that these men — they've
probably never heard the arguments of frogs round the pool at
night —

A: Into the twentieth century!

B: But then you see I only speak as a —

A: Savage — at best romantics —

B: While theirs of course is the voice of —

A: Common sense!

(*A and B freeze. C looks up and walks slowly forward.*)

C: And in my dream, I caught my breath and stood aghast — as the
court room agreed . . .

Bible notes

In the book of Genesis God gives creation into human care, but he does not then lose interest in it. After the story of the flood, God enters a serious covenant relationship, not just with the surviving human race but with all life on earth. Jesus himself draws lessons from God's detailed interest in the least of his creatures to encourage trust in his providence (Matthew 6:25ff).

Human care The Old Testament law is very detailed in its concern for animals and other aspects of the environment. The use of wild birds or trees for human needs is to be sparing and discriminating, and domestic animals should be well treated (Deuteronomy 22:4-6). In Nineveh, a city renowned for its wickedness, God had a concern for both humans and animals (Jonah 4:11). Proverbs sums it up as a mark of the 'righteous man' that he 'cares for the needs of his animal' — thus applying one of the strongest theological and ethical terms in the Bible to the most down-to-earth responsibility (Proverbs 12:10).

The earth is seen as being of special interest to God in the Old Testament; and a healthy, productive and cared for environment is a sign of God's blessing. For example, King Uzziah, who was one of the strongest and best kings of Judah, promoted farming in hitherto barren areas because, according to the Chronicler, 'he loved the soil' (2 Chronicles 26:10).

Future hope Christian hope is that, just as within the human personality there is the seed of that which will survive physical death, so within the created universe there is the God-given potential for renewal. The Bible speaks of judgement, which can be understood here as the direct result of human action: misuse of the environment literally brings destruction. But whatever the future brings there is always the possibility of rebirth.

Human beings as co-workers with God are responsible for the care of their environment which is part of the whole creation, and they can be involved in the process of renewal (Romans 8:18-23).

Follow up

Questions

1 What do you think the court case was about and who do you think won? Would you agree with this decision?

2 Ecology groups have grown in popularity over the past ten years. What relevance do you think what they say has to your life and the life of people in the Third World?

3 Is the concept of 'common ownership' a practical alternative in modern life?

Things to do

● Find out about any local land or other 'gift' ('common' or green belt for example) which has disappeared in living memory. (Local environmental or conservation groups might help, as well as older inhabitants.)

● Both CAFOD and Christian Aid* have resources concerning villages and other communities in developing countries who have lost their livelihoods because of the encroachment of industry onto their land or water.
Study this material and make a display for people to see.
*(For these and other addresses, see pp. 124-5.)

● Invite local representatives of environmental groups, business and politics to a 'Question Time' in your church.

Shall We Dance?

by Steve Stickley

Disease in the Third World is often a result of poverty and oppression. This active sketch is designed to attract and hold an audience's attention in a short space of time. It makes the point that we in the rich world are often more concerned with our own welfare than with the provision of basic needs elsewhere.

Characters   One (A documentary-style narrator)
Chorus (At least four people)

Stage directions
The chorus should be dressed in singlets and tracksuit bottoms. It should not be immediately obvious that they are in exercise gear but they should give the feel of a more neutral context.

Their chanting and movements need much rehearsal in order to build the climax effectively. The early movements can be determined by deciding on the exercises used at the climax and then working backwards, abstracting and minimalizing as you go.

The piece is suitable for adaptation into street theatre, remembering to re-inforce the statistics with large placards.

(*ONE is downstage. CHORUS are arrayed behind him already starting their ritualistic movements.*)

ONE: These natives need our help.

CHORUS: (*Chanting in rhythm with co-ordinated movements*)
lo-co, lo-co
hola-hola-mee-abra (*their movements continue throughout*)

ONE: They are ignorant of certain critical facts. Facts concerning life . . . and death.

CHORUS: lofa-chee, lofa-chee
nozza-mokka-inka-modda (*Clap twice*)

ONE: This ritual you see them performing is a simple Health Dance.

Their chants and gesticulations celebrate the food they
already have.

CHORUS: lo-co, lo-co
hola-hola-mee-abra

ONE: They call upon the sustainer of health to keep them well.

CHORUS: lofa-chee, lofa-chee
nozza-mokka-inka-modda (*Clap twice*)

ONE: However, the greatest need is one of education. How can we
help these natives to learn and understand the facts concerning health and welfare in the world?

CHORUS: lo-co, lo-co-la
hola-hola-meel-abra

ONE: Each doctor in their country is responsible for *six hundred and
fifty* people.

CHORUS: lofa-chee, lofa-chee
nose-a-mokka-inka-modda-aytun!

ONE: Only *thirty-nine pence* per day is spent on each of these
native's health care.

CHORUS: (*Their movements are gradually becoming recognizable as
fitness and aerobic exercises.*)
lo-co-la, lo-co-less
hola-hola-meel-abradda

ONE: For every one thousand people in their country, *twelve* will die
before they even reach their first birthday.

CHORUS: lofat-chee, lofat-chee
nose-amowka-rinka-modda-asian

ONE: They understand very little about the health care they
already receive in their country. The problem is, it's too good
to be true.

CHORUS: lo-co-less-low-cholestrol
hola-hola-wholemeal-bread
lofat-chee-low-fat-cheese
nose-amowka-rinka-modda-asian!

ONE: The name of their country? Britain.

CHORUS: (*Getting faster. Their movements are now recognizable as
familiar exercises.*)
low-co-less-low-cholestrol
hola-hola-wholemeal bread

> low-fat-cheese-low-fat-cheese
> no-smoking-and-drink-in-moderation! (*They stop, exhausted*)

TWO: I've had enough of that for one day.

THREE: Ha! We've only just started! (*They all flop down*)

ONE: So these native Britains relax from their rigorous Health Dance unaware that their obsession for survival and comfort blinds them to the simple need of a pure water supply for millions in the rest of the world. In fact . . .

THREE: Oi you! What are you doing?

ONE: (*Acknowledging interruption but forging on*) In fact, in Nepal there is only one doctor for every *thirty thousand* people.

FOUR: Leave him alone, he's only talking to himself. Come on, let's carry on.

ONE: Also in Nepal only sixty-six pence per *year* is spent on each person's health.

THREE: Hey you! Shut up will yer! You're a pain in the neck.

TWO: Come on, let's get going again. (*They chant and move as before. This continues to a climax.*)

ONE: (*Shouting above the noise*) In Bangladesh the infant mortality rate is *one hundred and thirty five* for every thousand people. In 1978 *twelve million* children died from malnutrition.

TWO: Put a sock in it!

THREE: Yeah, stop belly-aching!

CHORUS: (*Louder and more aggressively*)
> low-co-less-low-cholesterol
> hola-hola-wholemeal-bread
> low-fat-cheese-low-fat-cheese
> no-smoking-and-drink-in-moderation!

ONE: (*Increasing volume and urgency throughout the following*) The biggest problem is ignorance. Ignorance of the needs of others. Ignorance of how well-off we actually are! Ignorance of the unfairness of it all!

(*The CHORUS move en masse and slowly attempt to run ONE over. ONE backs off, bellowing . . .*)

ONE: Ignorance of our own responsibilities!

(*All freeze. The chanting ceases abruptly. Silent pause.*)

ONE: (*Softer, reasonable tone*) Shall we help these ignorant natives? (*Indicating chorus*) Or . . .
CHORUS: (*Heads turning to audience*) Shall we dance? (*They smile*)

Bible notes

The World Health Organization defined health as a 'state of complete physical, mental and social well-being, and not merely the absence of disease or infirmity' (*Alma-Ata* 1978). The Bible would agree with this, adding also the spiritual dimension, for it clearly shows that God's pattern for humanity is well-being in all dimensions of life. The spiritual dimension needs to be added because such total well-being is only possible when people are rightly related to God in love, trust and obedience. This is the full meaning of shalom in the Old Testament — much more than just peace or an absence of strife, it includes wholeness for the individual and in relationships.

Though health can be defined in broad terms, the popular use of the word relates primarily to the physical aspects of life, and there is considerable interest in it in the Bible. God's concern for the health of his people can be seen in the detailed laws for their social living which includes precautions for hygiene (Leviticus 11:32ff).

But ill health is not merely a physical thing, it is related to other aspects of life in which evil has become entrenched. Sickness can be a result of poverty which in turn is the result of oppression. Thus the battle for health is part of the wider conflict against evil in general.

The ministry of Jesus illustrated this clearly. His ministry of healing was not isolated but part of his total preaching and demonstration of the Kingdom of God. He was bringing the rule of God to earth and embodying its victory over all opposing forces of evil which weaken, sicken or enslave human beings in every dimension of life. His well-known words, 'Your faith has made you whole' underline the wholeness of his message and ministry for human bodies, minds, relationships with other people and with God.

The Bible's picture of a future age when God's Kingdom is fully established in the new creation very definitely includes 'health for all'. All crying, mourning and pain will be removed (Revelation 21:4).

Follow up

Questions

1 Does the health and fitness industry make a responsible contribution to people's well-being or is it just a money-spinner?

2 How highly do you value your health? If you were found to have a disease, how much would you be prepared to spend on treatment? On what would your decision depend?

3 Diarrhoea kills more children in the world than any other disease. It is usually caused by unsafe drinking water.
List the ways in which you would be affected if you did not have easy access to safe drinking water.

Things to do

● Write to the World Health Organization, CAFOD or Christian Aid for display material for your church or hall. (Addresses on page 124.)

● Arrange a showing of *Diagnosis Poverty, Lalibai* or *For Want of Water*. Each of these audio-visuals examines the advantages of small scale community based health programmes. *Lalibai*, a filmstrip, is particularly good for children.

● Consider all the medication, treatment or health aids that you use (e.g. tablets, glasses, physiotherapy, plaster, support bandages). Work out a system to tax yourself for each item used during one week. Try this as a group exercise. Give the money raised to overseas development work.

The Tea Shop

by Martin Williams and Roger Harington

Based on 'The Cheese Sketch', with grateful acknowledgement to John Cleese and Graham Chapman.

There are vast areas of the world where the nature of human labour has changed little from the ancient patterns of Biblical times. There are also societies where the conditions of allegedly 'free' employees are more harsh and oppressive than those of slaves in Israel. In such contexts the implementation of the Old Testament economic laws concerning work would be most beneficial. To introduce statutory rest days and holidays, statutory terms and conditions of employment, statutory protection from infringement of personal rights and physical dignity, together with statutory provision of fair wages promptly paid would revolutionize the face of economic life for millions of workers in such countries.

Unfortunately for them, various forces act against this, notably the 'middle men' — the landowners, agents and marketing executives. The ignorance of consumers of the conditions under which their purchases are produced is exposed in this sketch.

Characters   Customer
Shop assistant

Stage directions
This sketch requires only a counter and some recorded sitar music which is playing as the customer, a smart gent, enters. The shop assistant, who is friendly and sincere, stands behind the counter of the National Tea Emporium.

GENT: Good morning.

SHOP ASSISTANT: Good morning, Sir. Welcome to the National Tea Emporium, Sir.

GENT: Thank you my good man.

SHOP ASSISTANT: What can I do for you, Sir?

GENT: Well, I was just leafing my way through a little publication entitled 'How to bluff your way through One World Week'* in the Public Library a moment ago when I suddenly came over all dehydrated.

SHOP ASSISTANT: Dehydrated, Sir?

GENT: Mmm, arid, parched.

SHOP ASSISTANT: Eh?

GENT: Eee, I were all thirsty like.

SHOP ASSISTANT: Ah, thirsty.

GENT: In a nutshell. So I thought to myself a little infused foliage might do the trick. So I curtailed my bluffing activities, sallied forth, and infiltrated your place of purveyance to negotiate the vending of some oriental leaf.

SHOP ASSISTANT: Come again, Sir.

GENT: I want to buy some tea.

SHOP ASSISTANT: Oh sorry, Sir, I thought you were complaining about the sitar player.

GENT: Good heavens no. I'm one who delights in all manifestations of the Terpsichorean muse.

SHOP ASSISTANT: Sorry?

GENT: Eee, I like a nice dance, you're forced to.

SHOP ASSISTANT: So, he can go on playing then, can he?

GENT: Certainly. Now then, my good man, how about some tea?

SHOP ASSISTANT: Certainly, Sir. What would you like?

GENT: I'll take a quarter of Broken Orange Pekoe, if you please.

SHOP ASSISTANT: Ah, I'm afraid we're fresh out of the Pekoe today, Sir.

GENT: No matter. How are you on Keemun?

SHOP ASSISTANT: Er, never have it at the end of the week, Sir. Always have it fresh on Mondays.

GENT: Well then, stout yeoman, do you have any Lapsang Souchong?

SHOP ASSISTANT: Normally, Sir, but today the van broke down.

GENT: Not my lucky day, is it? Russian Caravan, Formosa Oolong, English Breakfast, Assam perchance?

SHOP ASSISTANT: Been on order two weeks, expecting it this morning.

GENT: Camomile, Rosehip, Royal Rose, Orange scented, Black-currant, Lime, Nestea Lift the Lemon Tea Mix?

*Can be altered to suit the occasion.

SHOP ASSISTANT: Try Morrison's, Sir.

GENT: Nuwara Eliya, Uva, Poona Candy, Dimbulla, Tetley, Brian Cohen Kosher Tea?

SHOP ASSISTANT: No, Sir.

GENT: Oivay, oivay, Jasmine?

SHOP ASSISTANT: Oh yes, Sir.

GENT: Oh good, you do have some of that. I'll have some then.

SHOP ASSISTANT: Well, it's a bit scented, Sir.

GENT: No matter, I like it scented.

SHOP ASSISTANT: Well, actually, Sir, it's very scented indeed.

GENT: Never mind, fetch hither le beau thé de la Chine.

SHOP ASSISTANT: Well actually it's a bit more scented than you like it, Sir.

GENT: I don't care how scented it is. Fetch it hither with all speed.

SHOP ASSISTANT: Oh dear.

GENT: What is it now?

SHOP ASSISTANT: The cat's done a whatsit on it, Sir.

GENT: Has he?

SHOP ASSISTANT: She, Sir.

GENT: Tish, tish. Mantunna, Black Lion, Jackson's Piccadilly, Taylor's Yorkshire Teabags, Pagoda, Ceylon Luaka, Twinings Nectar, Ronald Reagan Nuclear Cowboy Blend?

SHOP ASSISTANT: Stroll on, guv.

GENT: Lady Londonderry, Ginseng, Solidago, Penny Royal, Gunpowder Green Tea, Maggie's Falkland Hash? Do you actually have any tea?

SHOP ASSISTANT: Oh yes, Sir, we've got . . .

GENT: Don't tell me. I'm keen to guess. Queen Mary, Indian Prince, Mate Royal, Herbal Mint, Fennel Raspberry Leaf, Rooibosch, Earl Grey?

SHOP ASSISTANT: Oh yes, Sir.

GENT: Ah, splendid. You do have some Earl Grey?

SHOP ASSISTANT: Oh no, Sir. Not the tea, Sir. I thought you were talking to me. That's my name. Earl Grey.

GENT: Not much of a tea shop, is it?

SHOP ASSISTANT: It's the finest in the district, Sir.

GENT: Explain the logic, pray, underlying that conclusion.

SHOP ASSISTANT: It's so clean.

GENT: It's certainly uncontaminated by tea.

SHOP ASSISTANT: You haven't asked about the Darjeeling yet, Sir.

GENT: Is it worth it?

SHOP ASSISTANT: Could be.

GENT: Well, I'm game. Here goes. Have you got any . . . Shut that bloody sitar up . . . Have you actually got any Darjeeling, he said, expecting the answer 'No'.

SHOP ASSISTANT: Errrrr, no.

GENT: Walked straight into that one. Predictable really. It was an act of purest optimism to have posed the question in the first place. Right then, I'll take a packet of Cosy Brew.

SHOP ASSISTANT: Not much call for it round here, Sir.

GENT: Not much call for it? It's the most popular tea in Great Britain.

SHOP ASSISTANT: Not round here, Sir.

GENT: Well, what is popular round here, pray?

SHOP ASSISTANT: WDM special blend, Sir.

GENT: WDM Special Blend?

SHOP ASSISTANT: Oh yes Sir, World Development Movement Tea, Sir. Staggeringly popular in this manor, squire.

GENT: Is it?

SHOP ASSISTANT: It's our number one best seller, Sir.

GENT: And why isn't Cosy Brew popular, pray?

SHOP ASSISTANT: It's all these people with social consciences, Sir. They say they're not going to give their money to a firm that makes such huge profits and yet doesn't pay its workers enough. Do you know what the average tea worker earns, Sir?

GENT: I don't know. Something in the region of nine thousand pounds a year plus expenses and a company car I should imagine.

SHOP ASSISTANT: Shave off squire. More like forty pence a day.

GENT: Forty pence a day? Good heavens, man, you can't be serious.

SHOP ASSISTANT: It's perfectly true, Sir, and Cosy Brew and Multinational Sips to name but two of the main firms involved, made fifty million pounds profit last year, half of which came from their tea estate, so there you are.

GENT: But what difference will it make buying WDM tea. I bet it's just 'Do-gooders-ease-your-own-conscience' blend.

SHOP ASSISTANT: Oh very witty, Sir, I wish I'd said that.

GENT: You will, shopkeeper, you will.

SHOP ASSISTANT: But enough of this highly derivative material, Sir. Let me just tell you that the estate is owned by a trust that runs six homes for mentally and physically handicapped people and ten per cent of the price that you pay goes directly to help the workers and their families on the estate where the tea is picked.

GENT: Ten per cent?

SHOP ASSISTANT: You don't have to repeat it, Sir. I'm sure the audience got the detail the first time.

GENT: I dare say all this is true. But I'm not going to drink some filthy tea just to help a few wo . . . that is to say, coloni . . . I mean persons from abroad. I don't think I really care for this social conscience carry on.

SHOP ASSISTANT: But you haven't asked what sort of tea it is yet, have you, Sir?

GENT: Er, no.

SHOP ASSISTANT: It's the best quality Broken Orange Pekoe, Sir.

GENT: Do you mean to say you've had some Broken Orange Pekoe all this time?

SHOP ASSISTANT: Oh yes, Sir.

GENT: You've been deliberately wasting my time.

SHOP ASSISTANT: I haven't been wasting your time, Sir. I've been spinning out our little chat to educate you, Sir. I mean, you didn't know how much a Sri Lankan tea worker earned, did you Sir?

GENT: I can't say I did, no.

SHOP ASSISTANT: There you are then, Sir. All that useful information just for the price of a packet of the best quality Broken Orange Pekoe. I bet you wish you were better informed before you came in. Good day, Sir.

(*Gent exits in a hurry.*)

Bible notes

God is described in Genesis chapters 1 and 2 as a worker. So, made in God's image, we share in the work of creation through our purposeful activity. We are called to use our talents and resources creatively, and to enable others to do the same. To prevent somebody else from working, or to deny or deprive a person of work, is to offend against his or her humanity and against the image of God.

The Old Testament recognizes that work can be either fruitful and fulfilling or exploitative and frustrating. For this reason there is detailed treatment of the rights of workers including employers, hired workers, slaves and animals.

Hebrew slaves were to be given the opportunity of freedom after six years and their physical treatment was closely regulated. The wages of hired workers were to be paid fully and promptly on the day they were earned because, as in much of the world today, this is vital if a family's evening meal depends on the day's earnings. The prophets condemned the oppression and exploitation of labourers (Isaiah 58:3). Rest on the Sabbath was mandatory for employer, employees and even working animals, and the great festivals added extra breaks throughout the year.

All of this is supported in the New Testament. Paul gives clear instructions to employers and their slave employees about their attitudes and actions (Ephesians 6:5-9). James draws strongly on the language of the prophets as he attacks the rich for exploiting their workers (James 5:1-6).

Follow up

Questions

1 Is work a 'necessary evil' or basically a 'good thing'?

2 Are there people who are being exploited at work in this country? e.g. women, children, voluntary workers.

3 Would you be prepared to pay more for goods from the Third World if it meant the workers received a fair wage? Do you look out for examples of fair treatment of workers, for instance by buying through the CAFOD or Christian Aid catalogues produced by Traidcraft?

Things to do

- Ask the following how their paid work, or lack of it, affects their sense of their own worth in society: politicians, businessmen, housewives, unemployed, young, old, etc.

- Have a Traidcraft exhibition of goods from the Third World in your church. Their representative will explain about their policy on fair wages and buying.

- Christian Aid and CAFOD have information sheets on the working conditions on tea and coffee plantations in developing countries. Write off for these, and decide whether you could change your purchasing habits. (For these and other addresses, see pp. 124-5.)

The Pounds of the Castersugarvilles

A Highly Moralistic Melodrama

by Jo Rigarlsford and Roger Harington

No one today can claim ignorance of the fact that two thirds of the world's population goes to bed hungry or even starving. Yet feeding the hungry and asking why they are so is a basic Christian act. Jesus makes this a test of truly knowing and loving him, and it was a primary duty of the early Church.

By taking the topic of cash-cropping by multinational landowners, this sketch exposes one of the myths about self-sufficiency in the Third World.

Characters   Holmes
                    Watson
                    Butler

Stage directions
Watson should have a carnation in his button hole, and be holding a few photographs of an emaciated child. The Butler needs a tray on which are a banana, a carnation, a jar of coffee and a cotton reel. A sense of Victorian costume would help, viz: deerstalker, pipe, stick, cloak, etc. The piece is meant to be a melodrama, so the actors should work at building a good rapport with the audience.

It is worth noting that all the items on the tray can be 'murder weapons' in their own country.

WATSON: Good evening, Holmes.

HOLMES: Good evening, Watson. Watson . . .

WATSON: Yes, Holmes.

HOLMES: I notice you have some photographs in your hand, Watson, and this being One World Week*, I've a nasty feeling . . .

WATSON: How do you know it's One World Week*, Holmes?

*Can be altered to suit the occasion.

HOLMES: There are some very earnest people in the audience, Watson. So I've a nasty feeling that you're about to preach some morals to us.

WATSON: My guess is that you'll be the one who starts ruining the script by putting in a moral. You're the self-opinionated know-all around here.

HOLMES: Watson.

WATSON: Yes, Holmes.

HOLMES: Shut up. Now then, what are these photographs? Do they have something to do with a crime of some kind?

WATSON: They do indeed, Holmes. With murder.

HOLMES: With murder, Watson?

WATSON: I believe that is the kind of crime it is, Holmes. You see the child in this photograph, Holmes. He looks like one on a charity poster.

HOLMES: Why, Watson?

WATSON: Because he died of starvation, Holmes.

HOLMES: Why, Watson?

WATSON: Because he didn't have enough to eat, Holmes.

HOLMES: Why, Watson?

WATSON: Don't keep saying 'Why Watson?' to me, Holmes. It's a very boorish way of trying to make me lose my confidence. Anyway, why should I know why this child didn't have enough to eat?

HOLMES: I believe you should know, Watson.

WATSON: There, I knew you'd be the first to preach a message.

HOLMES: Watson.

WATSON: Yes, Holmes.

HOLMES: Allow me to unravel for you the mystery of the Pounds of the Castersugarvilles.

WATSON: Don't you mean the Hounds of the Baskervilles, Holmes?

HOLMES: No, Watson. I mean the pounds and pounds, and pounds and pounds, and pounds and . . .

WATSON: All right, all right.

HOLMES: . . . of the infamous multinational firm, Castersugarville, which owns many acres of sugar plantation in South America.

WATSON: That sounds pretty contrived to me, Holmes. You oughtn't to ruin the original story by putting in a moral like that. The audience won't like it.

HOLMES: This audience won't mind, Watson. They're into good causes. They expect to get bored. Listen, if I mistake not, here comes our client now.

(Enter a BUTLER with a tray, on which are one banana, one carnation, one cotton reel and a jar of coffee.)

WATSON: Oh no, Holmes. Not another murder when the Butler did it.

HOLMES: No, Watson. One of these objects is the murder weapon.

WATSON: You can't be serious, Holmes. One of these is the murder weapon? (*To the audience*) He's finally flipped his lid.

HOLMES: On the contrary, Watson. Now then, where does the child come from?

WATSON: It says here 'Colombia', Holmes.

HOLMES: Did you know, Watson, that in Colombia, like in many other countries, instead of the people being able to grow the food they need, they very often have to grow something else, because foreigners own the land?

WATSON: You mean the poor people of Colombia can't always grow what they want to grow because foreigners own the land?

HOLMES: You're wonderful, Watson.

WATSON: Holmes, I think I see what you're driving at. You mean the something else they have to grow is one of these four things on the tray, and can thus be considered the murder weapon?

HOLMES: Correct, Watson. Now then, where do bananas come from?

WATSON: I don't know, Holmes. I wasn't any good at Environmental Studies.

HOLMES: Have a guess, Watson.

WATSON: Jamaica?

HOLMES: No, she went of her own accord. Welcome to tonight's 'Oldest Joke in the World' contest. If you know a joke older than that —

WATSON: Keep it to yourself.

HOLMES: Right, where does cotton come from?

WATSON: I've no idea, Holmes.

HOLMES: I'll tell you, Watson. It comes from Paraguay.

WATSON: How did you know that, Holmes?

HOLMES: It says so on the reel, Watson.

WATSON: But I am the real Watson, and I never noticed.

HOLMES: Thank you, Watson. Don't call us, we'll call you. Right, so cotton isn't the weapon. Coffee?

WATSON: Oh, thank you, Holmes. White with one sugar.

HOLMES: No, you dumb cluck, where does coffee come from?

WATSON: Oh I know that, Holmes. Brazil. Where does this awful script come from?

HOLMES: Probably from Christian Aid/CAFOD.* Never mind, just hang in there a little longer and we'll come to the meaningful speech in a moment. So, coffee comes from Brazil. That means it can't be the murder weapon. Actually, it also comes from Colombia, but perhaps the readers of *The Guardian* and other pedants in the audience will forget that for the moment. So what are we left with?

WATSON: A carnation. A carnation? That's the murder weapon? I don't get it, Holmes.

HOLMES: Elementary, my dear wally, Watson. Rich people from other countries, like the Castersugarvilles, buy the land in Colombia, and then they can grow what they like, and pay very little money to those who work on the land . . . DON'T FALL ASLEEP WHEN I'M GIVING YOU THE MORAL, WATSON . . . carnations are very profitable and they're sold in Europe. The people in Colombia have very little land left to grow their own food, and very little money with which to buy food. The results you see in these photographs.

WATSON: Oh now I see. The carnation is the murder weapon. But Holmes, who is the murderer?

HOLMES: Who is wearing a carnation, Watson?

WATSON: Oh well, now look here, Holmes, I can't be held responsible. I'm not a murderer. I've never seen this child before.

HOLMES: That's what they all say, Watson. I won't arrest you, this time. But I do think you ought to go away and do some hard thinking, Watson. Especially when you next go into a florist's.

WATSON: I'll do that, Holmes.

HOLMES: I do so hope you will, Watson. Good night.

WATSON: Good night, Holmes. (*Exit HOLMES*)

WATSON: Patronizing Berk.

Bible notes

God gave all the resources of the earth to meet human needs. This includes the primary physical need for food. The gift is intended for sharing; it has been given to the whole human race.

Old Testament Israel was intended by God to be a model of a redeemed society displaying his justice and mercy in every area of life — personal and social. Even agriculture was included, special provision being made for the poor. Slaves had basic food rights, and necessities such as food or implements for preparing it were never to be exploited as security for a loan.

Such provisions in the law were made by God as an issue of basic justice, a reflection of God's own character. But the Bible is also realistically aware that human injustice can get in the way and produce a harsh contrast. Proverbs 13:23 observes that people are poor and hungry, not because of a shortage of food, but because of a shortage of justice (see also Amos 8:4-6) — something which those involved in development work would endorse.

Future hope The prophets painted a picture of a new world order with abundant food and drink achieved by God's justice. This is what lies behind the reference in the song of Mary, to God filling the hungry at the dawn of the new age when the Messiah was about to be born (Luke 1:53). It was also something that led people to recognize Jesus as the 'Prophet' when he miraculously multiplied food (John 6:14). For Jesus, food for the hungry was as much a sign of the Kingdom of God as forgiveness for the sinful.

Present obligation This messianic vision is more than a future hope. It is meant to challenge us to practical action now, working for justice, including the elimination of hunger. John and James make it a mark of genuine love and faith (1 John 3:17 and James 2:14-17).

Follow up

Questions

1 The food problem in the Third World is partly one of access to land. Good land is used by companies to grow food for export to the wealthy nations. Have you ever thought about where most of the food you eat comes from? Do you have any murder weapons on your shelves?

2 Dom Helder Camara, the former Archbishop of Recife, Brazil, has said, 'When I give food to the hungry they call me a saint. When I ask why the poor have no food they call me a communist.' Do you think our Christian calling to 'feed the hungry' stops us from asking questions?

3 What is the difference between 'Food Aid' and 'Development Aid'? Which would you support and why?

Things to do

● Organize a supermarket search to see how much multi-national companies dominate our lives. Visit a local supermarket and look through the commodities on the shelves; look for the brand names and parent companies on the labels. How many products can you find owned by a single company? What are the advantages and dangers of one company owning large ranges of products?

● Set up a 'rich/poor lunch' in your church or group to highlight affluence and poverty. Everyone pays a fixed amount for lunch, the majority receive bowls of rice, one or two have a three course meal. Draw lots to decide who gets what. Participants soon start to learn about inequality for themselves!

● Organize a multi-cultural evening of food, clothes and entertainment for your local church or group. Learn about the cultural traditions associated with food from around the world.

Water Fall

by Hugh Steadman Williams

'To each according to their need — not their greed.'

This attitude to ownership is rooted in the Christian principles of stewardship. The daily routine of our lives can be similarly judged. There is a morality of simplicity which is based upon our attitude to the possessions we have and to the acquisition of new ones.

For example — water. It would be wrong to say we should not be happy to have access to safe water supplies. But that joy should lead us to work to share the opportunity. In a very real sense the parable of Dives and Lazarus is applicable.

Characters   Suburban mother (some mime)
            Third World woman (mime only)

Stage Directions

This monologue with mime needs to be strongly caricatured with plenty of humour. It provides an opportunity for a talented performer with a good sense of timing.

Both women should be suitably dressed. The only props required are a tape recording of running water, the sound effect of a telephone ringing and a large pot or bucket to carry the water in.

Throughout the piece the Third World woman walks across or around the acting area carrying the large pot or bucket, if possible, on her head. The piece begins with the suburban mother miming the turning on of a tap and then washing a lettuce. When the telephone rings the tape of the sound of running water continues.

SUBURBAN MOTHER: (*Flat and brisk*) Hello. (*Pause*) Yes. Speaking. (*Suddenly bright, warm and welcoming*) Hello Tracey! Well I never. Nice to hear you! (*Pause*) Yes, isn't it. (*Pause*) Well, how *are* you? (*Pause*) I know. Ages. I was only saying to Richard the other day, before he went off on one of his trips, I said, 'It's funny but we haven't seen Tracey for ages.' And he said, 'Lost without trace!' Well, you know Richard. (*Pause*)

Noise? What noise? (*Pause*) Can't hear any noise. (*Pause*)
Oh, that. Yes, it's the tap running. (*Pause*) Yes, that's all. The
tap. Couldn't understand what you were on about. (*Pause*)
No, I don't need a plumber. Nothing to worry about. I'm just
washing some lettuce. For our tea. (*Pause*) I know. Aren't they
a price? But they're supposed to be good for you. Well, good for
me anyway, with my waistline. (*False laugh. Pause*) I don't
want to hear that word calorie ever again! (*Pause*) Do you?
Well I make a token effort. Just to please Richard. (*Pause*)
And our Vicar. (*Pause*) Well, you know him and his 'lunchless
lunches', or whatever they're called. How they help the starving millions beats me. I mean a lot of overweight women in a
draughty church hall fighting a losing battle against tummy
rumbles for two hours in the middle of the day, and putting
one pound fifty in the collection box for the privilege of doing
it. Half of them rush home and stuff their faces at tea time, I
bet you. (*Pause*) Oh it's something to do with sinking a bore
well. (*Pause*) I said a bore well. They want at least one in each
village. I mean how many lunches have I got to miss? (*Pause*)
Of course I want to help them. I remember what it was like
when we had that burst water main and we had to fill buckets
at a stand-pipe down the road. Fancy having to do that twice a
day for the rest of your life. But you've got to be realistic,
haven't you? I mean, missing too many meals might endanger
your health. Besides, I need to keep my strength up. (*Pause*)
It's all right for you. People like you can eat as much as you
like and still stay as thin as a twig. But me! I've only got to *look*
at a cream cake and I start to fill out. (*Pause*) Well, I know I
don't just look at them, you rude thing. (*Long pause*) Here,
hang on a minute before you tell me. I've just got to re-start the
washing machine. Won't be a sec.

(*In mime she puts down the phone and loads the front-loader, sets
the programme and pushes a button. She comes back to the phone
and picks it up.*)

(*Pause*) Sorry. Carry on. I'm all ears.

(*Silence as she listens to the latest gossip. In mime she reaches out for a glass. Puts it under the tap. Takes it away full. Takes a few sips, while still listening to the phone.)*

Of course I'm listening. (*Sips again*) No, it's not a bad line. It's me, having a sip. (*Pause*) No, it's not gin, either. It's just water. (*Pause*) Well, funnily enough I actually like the stuff. You should try it some time. (*Pause*) At least it's clean and healthy and doesn't cost anything. (*Pause*) Of course I've heard of water rates. But you know what I mean. (*Pause*) I know. Disgraceful aren't they? And now they're threatening us with meters. For water! I ask you. We ought to drill a bore well — in our garden. Then we could tell them what to do with their water meters. (*Pause*) How do you mean — regular Jack and Jill? Cheeky monkey! (*Pause*) Just a minute. (*Pause*) No, I thought I heard Geoffrey coming in. Yes, football this afternoon. He usually brings half the pitch back with him.

(*In mime she lowers the phone and puts her hand over it. Calls.*)

Geoffrey? That you? Well just be sure to wipe your feet! Put all your football things out for washing. And take a shower. Right now. Before you turn on the telly or do anything else. You heard me!

(*Back to the phone again.*)

Doesn't know what soap and water is, that boy. He wouldn't wash for a month if I didn't chase him. He'd just love your African drought, he would. Just the excuse he'd need. (*Pause*) Anyway, I must get on and get the tea ready. They'll all be home soon. (*Pause*) You've said it — at the trough with their tongues hanging out and their trotters over the edge. (*Pause*) Well, ta-ta for now. By-ee!

(*In mime she puts the phone back on the hook and returns to washing her lettuce at the sink. Still in mime she shakes the lettuce in the cullender and then takes it off to the dining room. The tap is still running.*

Now the lady with the water pot comes to a stop. She has reached the well. In mime she operates the pully and bucket, letting it down carefully. She hardly has the strength to wind it up again. With effort she lifts the bucket over the parapet of the well and empties the water into her pot. She lets the bucket into the well again. With great difficulty she manages to lift the pot onto her head. Then she turns and begins the long walk back home.

The sound of running, wasting, water continues.

Finally, after crossing the acting area several more times, she walks off, preferably through the audience, slowly wending her heavy way home.

Only when she is finally out of sight, and after a long pause, does the sound of running water fade away.

End of scene.)

Bible notes

Wealth and poverty are relative terms; few people will admit to being rich! Some Christians argue that wealth is a sign of God's blessing — so, the more the better. Others, throughout the history of the Church, have exalted poverty as the true vocation for followers of Jesus. Both opinions can use the Bible to support their argument.

Desirable but dangerous The Bible portrays God as infinitely generous, desiring abundance and plenty for all. Wealth can be a blessing (e.g. the patriarchs, Genesis 26:12ff), but at the same time it is clearly recognized that even blessings have dangers. Ecclesiastes 5:10-20 points to some of the absurdities and evils of wealth, but still affirms that work, wealth and possessions are God's good gifts to be enjoyed.

Damning differentials What the Bible does condemn is the display of wealth or excessive differentials between rich and poor. God's intention for Israel was a broad equality in which every family had its land. Even a king was not to acquire wealth in excess of his brothers (Deuteronomy 17:14-17).

But it is the prophets who make the most severe attack on excessive wealth in the presence of poverty, since they saw the one as the cause of the other. Amos (4:1) and Isaiah.(3:13-26) attack the luxury enjoyed by the women of Samaria and Jerusalem because such luxuries were paid for by the exploitation of the poor — whom the ladies in question possibly never encountered. Oppression is easier from a distance.

Enough is enough The basic attitude of the Bible to lifestyle is contentment with what is sufficient. In the teaching of Jesus, the mark of the truly godly lifestyle is trusting dependence on God and his ability to provide. It is that attitude which enables and frees us to seek more important things — 'the Kingdom of God and his righteousness' (Matthew 6:25-33).

The early Church lived by this teaching, abolishing differentials in their midst so that 'there were no needy persons among them' (Acts 4:32-35). Paul turned this into a principle for relationships between churches, the rich providing for the poor on the basis of equality. He based this teaching on the activity of God himself, who provided manna for his hungry people and saw to it that no one had less than enough, and no one had more than was needed.

Follow up

Questions

1 Do you think the character in the play is irresponsible about her attitude to, or her use of, water?

2 What do you think is the idea behind 'doing without', rather than just putting money in the collection plate?

3 Have you any experience of seeing somebody waste something you think you would have used more wisely? (E.g., money, talents, goods.)

Things to do

- Organize a 'tap-tax' for a week by agreeing to pay a fixed sum each time a member of your group or church uses a tap. Back it up with a display on 'Water'.

- Organize a 'water chain' or a water carrying procession through a busy shopping centre one Saturday to highlight the disparity between our easy access to water and the Third World problem.

- Suggest that your church conduct a 'Lifestyle Audit' and examine your private and corporate use of resources. (Schemes are available from the Boards of Social Responsibility of most Christian churches.)

Act 2

duration 7-14 minutes

Slave your Bacon

by Andrew Goreing

If you think that slavery is a thing of the past then think again. Hundreds of thousands of bonded labourers and exploited child workers are still being maintained as a virtually free labour force for landowners and manufacturers throughout the world.

In spite of laws to the contrary, some people still find it easy to trap their fellow human beings into economic and physical bondage. And we in the First World often benefit from this.

The abolition of slavery will only come when the welfare and needs of people take precedence over those of the economy — hopefully before pigs learn to fly.

Characters   Narrator
3 Chorus members

Stage directions

The narrator is, for the most part, slightly detached from the chorus, who switch scenes and characters rapidly.

Costumes should be simple, with hats or other items added to indicate particular characters. This sketch should be great fun for the audience. Props, which could be on a table or hat stand, include the following: trays and neck straps, items for sale as mentioned in the text of the play (or otherwise as available), a mock-up of a window frame, three dog leashes, a length of rope and a plastic knife. No particular set is required, but care should be taken to use the space available imaginatively.

NARRATOR: We want!
CHORUS: (*Together, punchy*) We want!
NARRATOR: We want to talk!
CHORUS: We want to talk!
NARRATOR: (*Conversational*) We want to talk about economics.
CHORUS: (*Yawn, tut, let-down noises, etc.*)
NARRATOR: We want to talk about one of the most remarkable of human institutions. The free market.

(*The* CHORUS *start scratching themselves all over. The* NARRATOR *watches for a few moments, nonplussed.*)

NARRATOR: *Free* market, not flea market.
CHORUS: Oh. (*They stop scratching*)
NARRATOR: (*Clapping his hands or ringing a handbell*) Market Day! Bring your goods! Buy and sell!

(*The* CHORUS *produce trays to sell their stuff from, like old-time match sellers.*)

CHORUS 1: Lovely oranges!
CHORUS 2: Flowers, lovely flowers!
CHORUS 3: (*Slight pause*) Stinking fish!
NARRATOR: Cotton dresses!
CHORUS 1: Hot muffins!
CHORUS 2: Motor cars!
CHORUS 3: Stinking fish!

(*The* CHORUS *freeze.*)

NARRATOR: The free market ensures: that demand and supply are balanced; that prices are kept as low as possible; that everyone gets a fair day's pay for a fair day's work; that the frog marries the princess and that —

(*He is interrupted.* CHORUS 1 *has been shading his eyes, peering into the distance stage left.*

CHORUS 1, 2 *and 3 go 'Oink oink, oink oink, oink oink' etc. starting very soft, rapidly getting louder.*

A large pig (*imaginary, if one can't be trained in time*) *flies across the stage at head height. The* CHORUS *all duck and watch it zoom past.*)

CHORUS 3: (*First to rise*) Pigs will fly.
CHORUS 1 AND 2: Oink oink! Oink oink!

(*The pig returns and catches* CHORUS 3 *on the side of the head with a trailing trotter.* CHORUS 3 *clutches at his head with a yelp.*)

NARRATOR: The market ensures that what society needs is produced as quickly and cheaply as possible.

(*CHORUS 3 ducks, then looks around in trepidation.*)

CHORUS 1: Lovely oranges!
NARRATOR: If you sell out soon — raise your output —
CHORUS 2: Hot muffins!
NARRATOR: Or raise your prices. If nobody wants your goods —
CHORUS 3: Stinking fish!
NARRATOR: Cut your production, or cut your prices.

(*Pause*)

NARRATOR: Come and buy! Come and sell!
CHORUS 1: Fifth generation micro-computers!
CHORUS 2: Nuclear-powered submarines!
NARRATOR: Drinking glasses with commemorative engravings of scenes from the wedding of the Prince and Princess of Wales including free plastic straw in the shape of the Archbishop of Canterbury!
CHORUS 1: Pedigree racehorses!
CHORUS 2: Mediterranean holidays!
NARRATOR: Self-assembly furniture!
CHORUS 3: (*Slight pause*) Several tons of very stinking fish!

(*Pause*)

CHORUS 1: Clothes pegs! (*Putting one on his nose*)
CHORUS 2: Aerosol perfumes!
CHORUS 3: (*Throwing away his tray in exasperation*) Problem! What do you do if you can't afford to buy anything?
NARRATOR: Sell something.
CHORUS 3: Got nothing to sell.
NARRATOR: We've all got something to sell.
CHORUS 3: (*Pulling out his empty pockets*) Not me.
NARRATOR: Sell your labour!
CHORUS 3: My labour? (*Thinks it over*)
CHORUS 1: Gold-plated Rolls-Royces!
CHORUS 2: Oil refineries!
NARRATOR: Movie studios! Pharmaceutical TNCs!
CHORUS 3: (*More quietly*) Odd jobs. Window cleaning. Spot of gardening.

NARRATOR: Of course! The market runs smoothly because we all want to *pay* as little as possible. But let's be honest, some of us — most of us — now and again, like to give for our goods rather less than they actually cost.

CHORUS 1: Excuse me?

(*CHORUS 3 produces a window-frame which he holds to frame his head and shoulders. With his other hand he slips a dog-leash around his neck and becomes a toy dog.*)

CHORUS 2: (*He is now a shopkeeper*) Yes?

CHORUS 1: How much is th- (*Stops dead*)

(*CHORUS 1 and 2 look at the dog.*)

CHORUS 2: Yes?

CHORUS 1: How much is that, erm — (*pause*) — er, how much is that doggy in the window?

CHORUS 2: (*Looking back at the dog. Fractional pause.*) The one with the waggly tail?

CHORUS 1: Yeh.

CHORUS 2: Parts five pounds, labour two pounds ninety-five pence.

CHORUS 1: I see.

CHORUS 2: Tax and national insurance contributions seven point six pence, depreciation on fixed capital fourteen pence, debt servicing three point five pence, twelve pence towards rent, four pence towards heating, lighting, workplace facilities, thirteen pence advertising and marketing costs, two pence distribution, fifty-five pence mark-up on average rate of profit, seventy pence retailers mark-up.

NARRATOR: Uh-huh.

CHORUS 2: Fifteen per cent purchase tax.

CHORUS 1: Give you a fiver for it.

NARRATOR: (*To audience*) You see?

CHORUS 3: Woof woof!

NARRATOR: And if there's something everyone likes to get cheap — it's other people's labour.

(*CHORUS 3 discards his window and doggy impediments.*)

NARRATOR: That's how it is in the free market. Or, as it was known in

the Ancient World —
CHORUS 3: The slave market.
CHORUS 1: What?
NARRATOR: One of the most remarkable of human institutions. The slave market.

(*CHORUS 1 and 2 wrap a rope around 3.*)

CHORUS 1: Two thousand denarii, that's my last offer.
CHORUS 3: Cheek.
CHORUS 2: Very reliable model. Well looked after. Only one old lady owner.
CHORUS 3: They're the worst.
CHORUS 1: Not much work left in him though.
CHORUS 2: Rubbish. Feel that. (*Pinching 3's biceps*)
CHORUS 1: (*Doing likewise*) Feel what?
CHORUS 2: The muscle!
CHORUS 1: (*Pinching 3 all over, trying to find the muscle*) No, can't seem to find . . .
CHORUS 3: Oh very funny.

(*CHORUS 1 yanks open 3's mouth and peers inside.*)

CHORUS 1: Useless.
CHORUS 2: No, they're safer without teeth.
CHORUS 1: Hmm.
CHORUS 2: Three thousand. I'm robbing myself.
CHORUS 1: No, he won't do.
CHORUS 2: Two for the price of one! I'll throw in this feller for nothing.
NARRATOR: Do you mind —

(*CHORUS 1 yanks NARRATOR's mouth open, peers inside, elbows him in the stomach, watches him double up, then lifts him up by the ear or hair.*)

CHORUS 1: What is this? Antiques Roadshow?
NARRATOR: Thankfully — (*wriggling free*) — slavery has been abolished.
CHORUS 3: We have Youth Training instead. (*Gets slapped on the head*)
NARRATOR: Thankfully — slavery has been abolished.

(The CHORUS *gather together, looking and pointing upwards, muttering to each other. The* NARRATOR, *after a moment of curiosity, wanders over to them. He looks up to see what they're looking at. Pause.)*

CHORUS: *(Together)* Oink oink oink oink oink oink . . .

NARRATOR: Well — when I say *abolished,* what I *mean* is —

CHORUS 1: It doesn't happen in Tunbridge Wells.

NARRATOR: No.

CHORUS 2: It *does* happen in Tunbridge Wells?

NARRATOR: No! It happens in other places, and under other names.

CHORUS 3: Youth Train — *(Gets slapped again)*

CHORUS 1: Don't say slavery — say a Job For Life.

CHORUS 2: The lesser leisure option for the dedicated labourer.

CHORUS 1: And no pension worries —

CHORUS 3: You work till you croak.

NARRATOR: Other names — like Bonded Labour. Time —

CHORUS 1: The present.

NARRATOR: Place —

CHORUS 2: Far from Tunbridge Wells.

NARRATOR: Dramatis Personae —

CHORUS 2: My name is Kismatiya.

CHORUS 3: Anjaneyula.

CHORUS 1: Kom bac than.

CHORUS 3: Jesus. *(Spanish pronunciation)*

CHORUS 2: From India.

CHORUS 1: Thailand.

CHORUS 3: South America.

NARRATOR: And the story goes something like this.

CHORUS 3: Mother!

*(*CHORUS 1 *and* CHORUS 2 *look at each other.)*

CHORUS 2: Oh very well. *(Puts a shawl over his head — probably best if* CHORUS 2 *is a man.)* Yes, my angel?

CHORUS 3: Mother —

CHORUS 2: My precious!

CHORUS 3: I'm getting married in the morning.

CHORUS 2: Idiot! Impossible!

CHORUS 3: I knew you'd be pleased.

CHORUS 2: I can't afford it.

CHORUS 3: Ask the moneylender.

CHORUS 2: He's a shark.

CHORUS 3: Then ask him politely.

CHORUS 2: Sir?

CHORUS 1: Next!

CHORUS 2: My son is getting married.

CHORUS 1: Congratulations. Not to a daughter of mine, I hope.

CHORUS 2: I need some money to pay for the . . . (*sourly*) celebrations.

CHORUS 1: How much?

CHORUS 2: Twenty pounds.

CHORUS 3: Twenty pounds?

CHORUS 2: Fifteen.

CHORUS 1: What can you offer as security?

CHORUS 2: Ah.

CHORUS 1: Do you have any assets?

CHORUS 2: Er, assets, no, I'm rather low on assets at the moment.

CHORUS 1: Any valuables?

CHORUS 2: Same with the valuables, really.

CHORUS 1: Any possessions at all?

CHORUS 2: Erm .

CHORUS 1: Do you have a house?

CHORUS 2: Well, I've got two sheets of corrugated iron and a cooking pot, if that's any good.

CHORUS 1: No assets at all.

CHORUS 3: You've got me!

CHORUS 2: We haven't come to liabilities yet.

CHORUS 3: I'm young, I'm strong, I'm a hard worker.

CHORUS 1: Does he ask questions?

CHORUS 3: Do I ask questions, mother?

CHORUS 2: Never.

CHORUS 1: He'll do. I need a good strong lad, preferably stupid. Let's talk about interest.

CHORUS 3: I'd like to travel and work with people.

CHORUS 1: Interest on the loan. Shall we say fifty per cent, or seventy? So, calculating your wages at six pence per day, minus necessary disbursements, expenses and professional remunerations, pension contributions and gift to the Sunshine Home for Distressed Moneylenders, that means you'll work off the debt in shall we say, sign here will you?

CHORUS 3: Oh.

(*CHORUS 1 takes 3's thumb, rolls it as if on an ink pad.*)

CHORUS 1: Twenty to er twenty five . . .

CHORUS 3: Days?

CHORUS 1: No.

CHORUS 3: Weeks.

CHORUS 1: Sign here.

CHORUS 3: Months?

CHORUS 1: No. (*Pressing down 3's thumb onto a contract*) There we are.

CHORUS 3: Twenty five years!?

CHORUS 1: I should start right away. (*Slips a dog leash over 3's neck*) Here. (*Hands 3 a plastic knife*) Chop me some firewood.

NARRATOR: Contemplating such scenes, we in the West react with sorrow.

CHORUS 1: With pity.

CHORUS 2: With outrage.

(*Pause. CHORUS 3 looks uneasily from side to side.*)

CHORUS 1: With indignation.

NARRATOR: Righteousness.

CHORUS 2: Compassion.

(*Pause. CHORUS 3 as before.*)

CHORUS 1: Anguish.

NARRATOR: With an iron determination to eradicate man's exploitation of his fellow man.

(*CHORUS 3 points up in panic. CHORUS breaks out into oink oinks.*)

NARRATOR: Let's run that last scene again. Time —

CHORUS 1: The present.

NARRATOR: Place —

CHORUS 2: Brazil.

CHORUS 3: Tanzania.

CHORUS 1: Mexico.

CHORUS 2: Nigeria.

NARRATOR: Dramatis Personae.

CHORUS 1: Brazil.

CHORUS 2: Tanzania.

CHORUS 3: Mexico.

CHORUS 1: Nigeria.

CHORUS 2: Thailand.

CHORUS 3: Sudan.

CHORUS 1: Indonesia.

NARRATOR: And the story goes —

CHORUS 3: Mother!

CHORUS 2: We need some money.

CHORUS 3: For development. For industrialization.

CHORUS 2: To modernize our agriculture.

CHORUS 1: Build up exports.

CHORUS 2: Foreign exchange.

CHORUS 1: We can't afford it.

CHORUS 3: Ask the moneylenders.

CHORUS 1: From the West.

CHORUS 2: You mean the banks.

CHORUS 3: Then ask politely,

CHORUS 1: Oi!

CHORUS 2: Sir!

CHORUS 3: Your honourable servant.

NARRATOR: How much?

CHORUS 1: Eighty million.

CHORUS 2: Say half a billion.

CHORUS 3: For the moment.

NARRATOR: What can you offer as security?

CHORUS 1: Ah.

CHORUS 3: Me.

CHORUS 2: Me.

CHORUS 1: Me.

CHORUS 2: Fifty millions.

CHORUS 3: Of our people.

CHORUS 1: Seventy millions.

CHORUS 2: Very hard workers.

CHORUS 3: Humble servants.

NARRATOR: I need a few million good strong lads.

CHORUS 3: The interest?

NARRATOR: I like to travel, and meet people. The usual interest. I'm sure we can work out a schedule to our mutual benefit. Just sign here.

(*As each signs in turn, with flourish and dignity, the* NARRATOR *slips a dog leash over their neck, and addresses a sentence to each.*)

NARRATOR: (*To* CHORUS 1) Grow me some coffee, would you?
(*To* CHORUS 2) Run me up a few shirts, there's a good chap.
(*To* CHORUS 3) Would you be interested in purchasing a nuclear power station?

(NARRATOR *tugs at the leash* — CHORUS 3 *nods: the others follow suit, nodding away like toy dogs on car back-window shelves.*)

NARRATOR: (*To the audience*) We want to talk about economics.

(*Blackout*)

Bible notes

We are tempted to look on the abolition of slavery as one of the major achievements of Western Christian civilization, forgetting not only that it was the same civilization that perpetrated the worst ever form of human slavery, but that in many parts of the world today virtual slavery still exists, in the form of child and bonded labour.

Although slavery was tolerated in Israel we should not dismiss the attitudes and laws of the Old Testament, since slavery did not by any means have uncritical approval. Israelites could never forget that they started out as a rabble of freed slaves from Egypt and this experience coloured their subsequent attitude to slavery. They could not subject one another to slave status or conditions, and their treatment of aliens in their society was to be marked with compassion and justice born out of the memory of Egypt where they had been denied both (Exodus 22:21; 23:9 and Deuteronomy 15:12-15).

The Bible suggests that slavery in Israel was not normally very harsh, most slaves being residential domestic workers who worked alongside the free members of society. The law gave slaves rights which were unparalleled in other ancient societies. They had legal protection from their own masters in the case of minor or fatal injuries (Exodus 21:20-26ff), and the law gave them the option of going free after six years service.

The most astonishing law in the Old Testament is the law of asylum which gave a runaway slave the right of freedom and residence in a village of his own choice — an opportunity unheard of elsewhere. This law was really a radical undermining of the whole institution of slavery itself. Slavery was clearly not regarded as something sacred or unchangeable. On the contrary, Israel's theology of a liberating God who created all human beings equal acted like a ferment in Israel's social structure which came to fruition much later.

Follow up

Questions

1 What do you know about slavery today? What examples could you give?

2 When does selling your labour become effective slavery?

3 Does slavery exist in this country today?

Things to do

● Work through specific material from CAFOD (*Slavery and Poverty*), Christian Aid or the Anti-Slavery Society and make a presentation to your church. (For these and other addresses, see pp. 124-5.)

● Many clothes are produced in sweat shops, mainly in Asia, which are then sold in High Street shops in the West. Organize a search for such clothes and use your local newspaper to highlight the injustice to the workers — often young girls of eight or ten years old.

● Ask if you can do a survey in your local school. Find out how many pupils have a job outside school hours. How many hours do they work and how much are they paid? Who benefits most out of this form of child labour, the workers or the employers?

Borrowed Time

by Neal Mason

There is a big difference between the debt which we willingly incur in order
to obtain some luxury and one which we necessarily incur in order to live.
The Old Testament Laws strongly protect the person who goes into debt
through uncontrollable circumstances and poverty. However, modern
banking terms, both on a national and international level, do not include
these moral safeguards. As Richie says in the sketch, '. . . this is a
business, not a charity'.

The characters can be seen either as themselves or as representing the
richer and poorer worlds, the North and the South. The setting of a local
loan company could just as easily be an international bank boardroom.
And while the borrowing nations may not be as gullible as Mrs Small, they
are frequently as powerless.

Characters   Clive Britain (Trainee Manager)
                Richie   (Experienced Manager)
                Mrs Small   (Debtor)

Stage directions

The main item of furniture is a counter, with a sign which says 'The
Multinational Loan Co.'. Behind the counter stands a desk with a ledger
and various official forms on it. Clive Britain, dressed in a suit, stands
behind the counter. Richie's cynicism is casual, almost good-humoured.
However, to begin with, he enters, slouches towards the counter and
employs an uneducated voice.

RICHIE: How do I go about a loan then?

CLIVE: Good morning. There's a simple form to fill in.

RICHIE: Go on then.

CLIVE: (*Taking a form and pen*) If you'd just write your name and
address in the space provided — block capitals please.

RICHIE: (*Writing*) Does it take long? Only I need the money a bit
smartish.

CLIVE: It's quite a quick process. (*Taking back the form and pen*) I'll need to take a few details from you, Mr — (*reading*) Danegeld is it?

RICHIE: That's it. Fire away.

CLIVE: How old are you, Mr Danegeld?

RICHIE: Twenty-eight.

CLIVE: Occupation?

RICHIE: Brain surgeon.

CLIVE: (*Giving him a look*) How long in present employment?

RICHIE: Forty-five years.

CLIVE: Oh come on, Richie! How do you expect me to learn the job if you don't take this seriously?

RICHIE: (*In his natural, refined voice*) You have to learn the dodges, Clive — or wasn't I subtle enough?

CLIVE: Mr Danegeld indeed!

RICHIE: Well, it's appropriate; once you pay loan companies, you never get rid of them. Anyway, you're doing well for your first day. Carry on.

CLIVE: Right; how much did you want to borrow?

RICHIE: (*Uneducated voice*) An 'undred quid.

CLIVE: (*Writing*) One hundred pounds. Now, I'll need details of your earnings and outgoings.

RICHIE: (*Refined voice*) OK Clive, we'll skip those for the moment; assume you've got them.

CLIVE: Mr Danegeld, have you any County Court Judgements against you?

RICHIE: (*Uneducated voice*) Oh, dozens: bad debts, embezzlement, fraud — oh and one for indecent exposure.

CLIVE: What!

RICHIE: (*Refined voice*) Well, I'm hardly likely to volunteer such information, am I?

CLIVE: There's no point in asking the question then.

RICHIE: None at all. When you do a search with the local Trade Protection Society, you'll soon find out whether I'm a bad payer — which is quite likely if I live on the Sahara Estate.

CLIVE: The local slums?

RICHIE: A sort of Sudan of the suburbs. Squalid. Low income.

CLIVE: So we refuse their loan applications?

RICHIE: On the contrary; how else do you think we make a profit?

And if they misuse the loans — blow it all on a knees up or something — that's *their* lookout. So long as they pay.

CLIVE: Will you be at home this evening, Mr Danegeld?

RICHIE: (*Uneducated voice*) What's it to you?

CLIVE: I'll have to visit you. For one thing, I need to see evidence of your income — recent payslips.

RICHIE: (*Refined voice*) Don't forget their payment books — H.P., rent etc. Look at the dates and see how promptly they've paid. Get chatting and listen for anything incongruous — unexpected bills for a car they haven't got. Things like that.

CLIVE: OK. Now, on a hundred pound loan, you'd have to repay five pounds a week for twenty-eight weeks. We'll need to be sure you can keep up the payments.

RICHIE: Right. Now I give you a hundred and one reasons why I can keep up the payments.

CLIVE: Don't they flinch at the prospect of paying back a hundred and forty pounds? That's forty per cent in about six months.

RICHIE: Yes, cheap isn't it?

CLIVE: Cheap!

RICHIE: You ain't seen nothin' yet, as they say.

CLIVE: You mean it gets even more expensive?

RICHIE: Somewhat. Clive, these people are hardly in a position to cavil; they can't afford *not* to take our money. Besides, we rely on their ignorance. Just hope, for your job's sake, no one publicizes how we operate.

(MRS SMALL, *who has a local, uneducated accent, enters and approaches the counter.*)

RICHIE: Ah, Mrs Small. I was coming to see you today.

MRS SMALL: It's about last Friday's payment —

RICHIE: (*Moving behind the counter*) It's unlike you to miss one, Mrs Small. When the collector told me, I could hardly believe it. But, as I was just saying to Mr Britain here, I knew you'd be back.

MRS SMALL: I intended to pay, but I couldn't. That's what I'm here about.

RICHIE: What's the problem?

MRS SMALL: It's a bit . . . personal.

RICHIE: Don't worry about Mr Britain; he's going to be your new branch manager.

CLIVE: Pleased to meet you.

MRS SMALL: You leaving us then?

RICHIE: New horizons, Mrs Small. I'm opening a branch in Wolverhampton. Now, your problem.

MRS SMALL: What happened — why I didn't pay — it's my daughter. She's pregnant. (*Upset*) I don't know which way to turn. She didn't even say — it was the headmistress who told me — morning sickness — and the boy doesn't want to know. We had a terrible bust up over it — she stormed out — chucked her part-time job. I can't cope — both my sons are out of work — I can hardly even pay for food. I mean, it was all so sudden, such a shock, what with the bills as well. I can't see any end to it.

RICHIE: Don't upset yourself, Mrs Small. I'm sure we can sort something out. Mr Britain, would you fetch the repayment ledger.

(*CLIVE brings the ledger from the desk and thumbs through the pages.*)

MRS SMALL: I don't know what to do — I just want her back home — well, I've got to stick by her —

RICHIE: Of course you have.

CLIVE: Small. Yes, here we are.

RICHIE: Let's see now.

MRS SMALL: Is it all right if I miss this week's payment?

RICHIE: I think we can do better than that for you. You say you can't manage —

MRS SMALL: I can't.

RICHIE: So how would it be if I gave you twenty pounds?

MRS SMALL: Twenty pounds? How do you mean?

RICHIE: Let me explain. You had a hundred pound loan.

MRS SMALL: Yes.

RICHIE: And you've paid twenty-two weeks; that's a hundred and ten pounds. That means you owe us thirty pounds. Right?

MRS SMALL: Six weeks left. Yes, thirty pounds.

RICHIE: Now, what I can do for you is reschedule your debt. First, we cancel your old loan — we wipe it out.

MRS SMALL: What, completely?

RICHIE: Completely. But I give you a new loan for fifty pounds. Deducting the thirty you owe us, that means I give you twenty.

MRS SMALL: You'll give me twenty?

RICHIE: But the good part is, you begin a new twenty-eight week repayment period; and the weekly payment on a fifty pound loan is only two pounds fifty.

MRS SMALL: But I've been paying five.

RICHIE: Pretty generous eh? Not only do you receive twenty pounds, but you halve your weekly payment. However, if I do this for you, I want your assurance you'll cut down on unnecessary expenditure — fewer expensive foods like meat, for instance.

MRS SMALL: Oh I will, I promise.

RICHIE: That's settled then. Mr Britain, fill in a promissory note would you.

(*While* CLIVE *writes,* RICHIE *takes money from a cash box.*)

MRS SMALL: (*Relieved*) You don't know what a load you've taken off my mind.

RICHIE: We look after our valued customers, Mrs Small.

CLIVE: Mrs Small, would you sign here please. (*MRS SMALL signs.*)

RICHIE: There. Everyone's happy. It's even saved me a journey to your factory.

MRS SMALL: (*Alarmed*) The factory? You wouldn't visit me at work?

RICHIE: Of course not. Unless it was absolutely necessary.

MRS SMALL: But if they — it's nothing to do with them —

RICHIE: Exactly. It's just that I didn't want to miss you at home. Anyway, it's not a problem — so long as you pay the collector every Friday.

MRS SMALL: Oh, I will. Is that my money?

RICHIE: All yours. Except we deduct last week's payment from it; that's a five pound debt you needn't worry about.

CLIVE: But Richie —

RICHIE: And we'll take off the first payment — two pounds fifty — so you needn't pay till next Friday. Then there's the usual one pound stamp duty.

CLIVE: Stamp duty? Surely that doesn't apply?

RICHIE: An administration cost, Clive. (*Laughing*) Mrs Small knows more about it than *you* do — isn't that right, Mrs Small?

MRS SMALL: I'll be an expert soon.

RICHIE: That's true! (*Counting out money*) Here we are then; ten, eleven, eleven pounds fifty. Happy now?

MRS SMALL: Thank you. I was so worried — I can't tell you.

RICHIE: Goodbye then. Don't miss the collector on Friday.

MRS SMALL: (*Leaving*) I won't, I promise.

(*MRS SMALL leaves. CLIVE scribbles on a piece of paper.*)

RICHIE: Another satisfied customer. What are you writing?

CLIVE: Just doing some rough sums.

RICHIE: Most of them are as docile as that. You get the occasional stroppy one who wants a fight, but not often. The thing is, renewals like this help to achieve our lending targets. (*Pause*) What rough sums?

CLIVE: Do you realize she's paying over sixty per cent per annum on the money she's received?

RICHIE: Is that all? Peanuts. I wouldn't even like to *guess* the rate for someone who renews loan after loan.

CLIVE: You mean some of these accounts have been going on for years?

RICHIE: Aeons.

CLIVE: And it's legal?

RICHIE: Of course. No one forces them.

CLIVE: Suppose they all defaulted at once?

RICHIE: We'd go bust. But it's hardly likely. As for the promissory notes, they're hardly worth the paper they're printed on. The point is, the punters *think* they are. We threaten to take people to court occasionally, but we never do — we're hardly in a position to. Besides, we don't exactly want to advertise what we're doing; there'd be a public outcry.

CLIVE: I see. With all the profit you make, surely you could afford to write off the debts of the poorest? Those who can barely afford to eat.

RICHIE: Easily. But this is a business, not a charity. Now, on with the lesson. This time *you* be the punter; invent a situation and watch how I handle it.

CLIVE: OK.

(*CLIVE withdraws from the counter, then approaches like a customer.*)

RICHIE: Good morning. How can I help you?

CLIVE: I saw your ad' in the paper. About loans. I'd like to apply for one.

RICHIE: If you'd just write your name and address on this form.

CLIVE: (*Writing*) I need the money rather urgently. There you are, block capitals.

RICHIE: Fine. (*Taking the form*) I'll need to take a few details from you, Mr — (*reading*) Reporter? You dog, Clive! You're up to *my* tricks! What kind of name's *that*?

CLIVE: It's no worse than Danegeld.

RICHIE: I suppose not. All right; how old are you, Mr Reporter?

CLIVE: Twenty-eight.

RICHIE: Occupation?

CLIVE: Reporter.

RICHIE: How long in present employment?

CLIVE: Three years. Ever since my newspaper began exposing sharp practices.

(*Pause. RICHIE looks at CLIVE.*)

RICHIE: (*Laughing uncertainly*) Yes, very good. Like it.

CLIVE. (*Laughing*) Good. I'm glad you see the funny side of it. (*Seriously*) You haven't bought a house in Wolverhampton, have you Richie?

RICHIE: (*Sobered*) What?

CLIVE: Only I've a feeling jobs round there are hard to come by.

RICHIE: (*Laughing nervously*) When I said invent a situation — you're a sly one! You almost had me convinced!

CLIVE: (*Seriously*) As I say, you might find work hard to come by. (*Making to leave*) I do hope you don't have to resort to borrowing money.

RICHIE: A . . . reporter? Clive, wait! Where are you going?

CLIVE: Back to work, Richie. To write it up. Publicity — remember? The one thing, with all your money, you can't afford.

(*CLIVE faces RICHIE, pauses, then leaves. RICHIE stares after him as the lights fade out.*)

Bible notes

When debt is referred to in the Bible it is usually incurred to obtain basic necessities such as a loan of seed corn for a farmer to produce next year's crops, or foodstuffs to support the family until the harvest.

In this context, the most basic feature of the Old Testament economy was the prohibition on taking interest on any loan to a fellow Israelite (Exodus 22:25, Leviticus 25:35-38). The point of this law was to prevent people from taking unscrupulous advantage of someone in trouble. Poverty and debt are affliction enough without others adding to them for their own gain. Not taking interest was so important that it was seen as a mark of a righteous person (Psalm 15:5).

However, even without interest, a loan was still a loan and the Bible recognizes the social and economic reality of debt as well as its evil. So it sets out a number of regulations which tried to mitigate its worst effects.

1   A creditor was not allowed to seize as security anything which was vital for the life or health of the debtor, such as clothing or domestic millstones.
2   The debtor retained personal rights such as the privacy of his home and could not be treated harshly as a slave (Leviticus 25:39-43).
3   All debt was subject to sabbatical laws of release on the seventh year and cancellation at the Jubilee. This included land, pledges given in debt and dependent persons.

The main purpose of these laws was to prevent the debt of one generation being passed on to the next — which is one of the main causes of poverty in some countries today, especially in rural areas. The idea was to enable people to get back on their feet with a fresh start — not just charitable short term assistance.

Israel was constantly falling short of these ideals, and the prophets showed great anger at the abuse of the debt laws.

Jesus himself used the language of the Jubilee to characterize his ministry (Luke 4:18). He called for a radically different attitude towards possessions in general which certainly affected the issue of loans and debts (Matthew 5:42). He used the same word both for spiritual forgiveness of sins and release from material debts (cf The Lord's Prayer, Matthew 6:12).

Follow up

Questions

1   Which character in the sketch did you identify with and why?

2   What is the difference between incurring debt for luxuries and incurring debt for necessities? What is your own experience of debt? What would you advise people to do if they are considering loans for necessities?

3   Many Third World countries say that, particularly since the mid 1970's, they cannot afford to pay the interest on their loans.
    What do you think should be done?
(If these questions are used for group discussion, leaders might like to have available statistics from CAFOD's *Debt and Poverty* or *Debt — New Deal for the Poorest*, a paper from the World Development Movement. For addresses, see pp. 124-5.)

Things to do

●   Have you ever heard about Credit Unions? There is a British Association which will give you details. This is a real way to find a community answer to local indebtedness. (Address on page 125.)

●   Do you have experienced members of your church who might be able to give free advice to people like Mrs Small? (E.g. accountants, solicitors, senior managers.)

●   Where would be a good place to show this play again? Could you invite certain people like your M.P. or local Bank Manager for a discussion afterwards?

Restoration Tragedy

by Andrew Goreing

'The highest heaven belongs to the Lord, but the earth he has given to man' (Psalm 115:16). 'The earth is the Lord's and everything in it' (Psalm 24:1). These two verses sum up the two sides of the Biblical view of the earth and its resources, of which the land itself is the greatest. On the one hand God has given the earth to mankind for sharing and use. On the other hand, God is still the owner, and this should determine *how* we share and use the earth. Questions of ownership, distribution, access and use of land are therefore not only economic but also moral.

This sketch presents the feelings of many people who do — or at least, did — make their living from the land. For these people a statement like 'the land is our mother' has real significance. Our own culture often loses sight of this reality. The sketch brings home the problem of one person's greed for land and the misery it creates for a community.

Characters   Narrator
                 Peasants (at least four)
                 Landowner

Stage directions
The play needs several props including a wheelbarrow, a sack full of soil or sand, a gun and various pots, seed trays, an egg cup, a coin and a long piece of paper to be used as a document. There is also the need for special bell and klaxon sound effects, which could be on tape, live or created by voices.

(*The* NARRATOR *enters. He* (*or she*) *is dressed in rough working clothes and is carrying a sack of earth or sand. He puts down the sack and addresses the audience.*)

NARRATOR: Once upon a time the land was the common heritage of men and women. Whatever your family could farm, or your tribe could hunt, or your clan's cattle could graze — that was your land.

    You shared it with the beasts and the plants. You held it in trust for your children. The land was precious. You cared for it, you protected it. You wove spells above it. Perhaps you pacified it with magic and sacrifice.

(*NARRATOR opens the neck of the sack.*)

NARRATOR: We read in the Bible that the land belongs to God. All the earth is his. But the land he gives to his people, for them to be the stewards of it.

(*The Peasants enter, one by one, and approach the NARRATOR. During the next speeches they receive the earth, poured from the NARRATOR's hands into their hands. They take away their handful of land and pour it into flowerpots, seedtrays, bowls, jugs and any appropriate domestic items.*)

NARRATOR: Every family that lived in the country had land to farm. Some had small plots, some had large. Everyone had enough, so that no one should be poor.

Every year the round of seedtime and harvest, of tending and grazing the flocks. Every seventh year the land was to have its sabbath. It must lie fallow and rest. The harvest of the sixth year must be enough for two years.

The land could be bought and sold. A rich man could buy several plots. But after the seventh of the sabbath years — every fiftieth year — all land was to be returned. It was the Year of Restoration.

The land was restored to its original owners, or to their descendants, so that no one should be poor.

(*One of the Peasants offers a pot to the NARRATOR, who takes it in his hand.*)

NARRATOR: What is land worth? It is worth the value of the crops it will bear. (*To the Peasant*) What do you grow?
PEASANT: Barley.
NARRATOR: How many years is it till the Year of Restoration?
PEASANT: Six years.
NARRATOR: This land is worth the six harvests of barley. (*Hands the pot back*)
(*To all*) Deal justly. Protect the weak. Look after the land.

(*As he retires or departs*) Of course, different times, different customs.

(*The Peasants work — e.g. water their crops, form a line for hoeing. Enter the* LANDOWNER; *a neat-looking man, carrying an egg cup.*)

LANDOWNER: Hi!

(*The Peasants straighten up*)

PEASANT A: Hallo.

LANDOWNER: I — er — um — hear there's some land to be had.

PEASANT A: That is right.

LANDOWNER: (*Approaching the sack, holding up his egg cup, smiling ingratiatingly*) And one just — helps oneself? As it were?

PEASANT B: Take what you need.

PEASANT C: It doesn't belong to anyone.

PEASANT B: We all share it.

LANDOWNER: And what perfectly charming little farms you all have. Erm — (*Pokes doubtfully at the earth; brushes the dirt daintily from his fingertips*) — you don't have a pair of gloves, do you?

PEASANT A: (*Comes to the sack, plunges in his hands and takes some earth*) We push back the jungle and put more land under the plough. It is hard work. Slow work. Our hands get dirty. (*He goes back and shares the earth with the other peasants*)

LANDOWNER: Well — I'm prepared to work as hard as anyone.

(*He tosses his egg cup away, strides off stage and returns with a wheelbarrow. The Peasants are hoeing with their backs to him and do not see. The* LANDOWNER *surreptitiously empties the sack into his barrow and wheels it aside. He sits beside it, pulls his hat over his eyes and snoozes, or whistles nonchalantly.*

A Peasant goes to the sack and finds it empty. He approaches LANDOWNER.

A din of bells and klaxons. LANDOWNER *snaps into readiness and aims a gun at* A.)

LANDOWNER: Who's there? What do you want?

PEASANT A: What has happened?

LANDOWNER: You're trespassing!

PEASANT A: There is a fence around the land!

LANDOWNER: Get away!

(*PEASANT A retreats. NARRATOR returns and picks up the empty sack, and watches.*

The Peasants squat by their holdings, perhaps humming sadly. LANDOWNER gets up, takes his barrow, and moves around the stage to the first Peasant he comes to.)

LANDOWNER: Buenos días.
PEASANT B: Señor.
LANDOWNER: How's things?
PEASANT B: Very bad.
LANDOWNER: Tut-tut-tut.
PEASANT B: This year the crops are not so good.
LANDOWNER: You could do with some money?
PEASANT B: Señor.
LANDOWNER: (*Tossing him a coin*) I'll buy your land.
PEASANT B: It is worth more —
LANDOWNER: Market's depressed. Toss it in.

(*B empties his pot into the barrow.*)

LANDOWNER: (*Inspecting B's pot*) Keep that for your vegetable patch.

(*He moves on to PEASANT C.*)

PEASANT C: Señor.
LANDOWNER: I'll give you five bob for it.
PEASANT C: How am I to live?
LANDOWNER: My dear man! — I'll give you a job.
PEASANT C: Señor is very kind.
LANDOWNER: Yes. Report at the farm at six a.m.

(*He moves on to PEASANT A.*)

PEASANT A: My land is not for sale.
LANDOWNER: Certainly not!
PEASANT A: Good.
LANDOWNER: It belongs to me already.
PEASANT A: What do you mean?
LANDOWNER: You have heard of my many evil deeds?

PEASANT A: Of course.

LANDOWNER: This is one of them. (*Producing a document which unrolls, toilet-roll fashion, to the floor*)

PEASANT A: You are a cheat.

LANDOWNER: Nonsense. *This* is the law, and *this* (*picking up A's land and tossing it into the barrow*) — is the profits.

(*LANDOWNER returns home, stopping for a second at the NARRATOR and his sack.*)

LANDOWNER: Put that down. People have no respect for property these days. (*He reaches home and sits down again.*)

(*The NARRATOR wanders over to him and idly runs his fingers through the soil in the barrow.*)

NARRATOR: You have much land.

LANDOWNER: Ah! God is good, Señor!

NARRATOR: Indeed he is. How did you come by so much?

LANDOWNER: It has been in the family for generations. My great-grandfather was a pioneer. When this was virgin land he came with his barrow, and set up his homestead, and cleared the jungle with his own hands.

NARRATOR: He was the first man here?

LANDOWNER: How else did I come to inherit all this? Of course, there were some Indians maybe. And a few peasants, that is all. They were eager to sell, they only live for gold.

NARRATOR: Perhaps these people are their descendants.

LANDOWNER: I think so, perhaps.

NARRATOR: They are very poor.

LANDOWNER: Señor, some people are rich, some people are poor. What will be, will be.

NARRATOR: Some are thieves and some are honest men.

LANDOWNER: No, our peasants are mostly good people. They give us very little trouble. Good day señor.

(*The NARRATOR flings a handful of soil at the LANDOWNER, then siezes him by the wrists.*)

NARRATOR: Strange that your hands remain so clean.

(*Bells and klaxons. The* NARRATOR *goes to the Peasants and squats with them.*)

LANDOWNER: (*Jumping up*) Saboteur! Radical! Guerilla! Termite!

NARRATOR: The Holy One, blessed be he, he has scattered the proud with all their plans, he has brought down the mighty from their high places, and lifted up the lowly, he has filled the hungry with good things and sent away empty-handed the rich.

LANDOWNER: (*Pause*) Marxist!

NARRATOR: Believe me, a day of restoration is coming.

LANDOWNER: Over my dead body!

NARRATOR: My friend — I hope not.

(*Blackout.*)

Bible notes

God's promise to Abraham included the promise of land for his descendants (Genesis 15:18ff). Later, the Exodus explicitly took Israel out of a state of landless economic oppression into a land of their own. The major feature of their new system of land tenure was equity — in simple terms, 'fair shares for all' (Numbers 33:53ff). Tribal allocations were made according to the size and need of the tribe, and the repeated phrase 'according to their clans/families' shows that the division of land was meant to give a share to every household unit (Joshua 13-19).

This system was in deliberate contrast to the preceding Canaanite system in which local kings owned all the land and everyone else was a serf. In Israel priority was given to the ordinary populace and economic viability was ensured for every household by giving each a fair share in the national asset — God's gift of land.

The system was then protected by two other principles.

1 *Inalienability of land*   Land was not to be bought and sold outside the family. This protected the interests of future generations.

2 *Redemption*   If land had been surrendered out of need (e.g. poverty or debt) it was the duty of the better off kinsman to retain it for the family. At the Jubilee, land reverted to its original owner. So in practice, when land was sold it was really only rented for a number of harvests until the Jubilee Year (Leviticus 25: 8-28).

Most societies today lack the strong kinship-land bonds that existed in Israel. In applying Biblical principles we cannot merely imitate Israel, but it does provide a model for objectives and priorities with regard to land, these are:

1 The need for access to and use of land should be recognized as well as the right of legal ownership. God is the ultimate owner and humans are fellow tenants of a common earth.

2 Wide distribution of land is preferable to concentration in the hands of a few.

3 The economic interest of every household unit should be the prior concern of any system or projected reform of land ownership. Israel's system was geared to the economic health of the lowest, not the elite in their community.

Follow up

Questions

1 'Primitive' and 'developing' cultures have a very close affinity with the land. What is your feeling for and connection with the land, and what do you think of theirs?

2 Should the use of land (things like 'Green Belt', the Amazonian rain forests, desertification) be an issue for the Church and Christians?

3 What might be a modern equivalent to sharing out the land according to Biblical principles?

Things to do

● CAFOD and Christian Aid can provide you with details about the use and abuse of land. Posters, pictures, case studies and information are available. Make up a display for your church and link it to a special occasion, such as Harvest Festival. (For these and other addresses, see pp. 124-5.)

● Many multinational companies have bad records in dealing with the land in Third World countries but have good reputations in Europe. You could buy shares and then ask questions at shareholders' meetings. The World Development Movement have experience in this sort of activity and can give you advice. (Address on page 125.)

● Arrange to show to a church meeting one of the films, videos, or sets of slides from Christian Aid or CAFOD, for example: *Exiles in their own Land* (landlessness in Brazil); *Bargain Buy* (food production). Full details are given in respective resource catalogues. (For these and other addresses, see pp. 124-5.)

ACT 3

duration 15-20 minutes

Political Prisoners

by Alan MacDonald

The Bible affirms that God is actively interested in the human social order. Throughout, God's severest judgements are on those who, though entrusted with political authority and care for the rest of society, fail to live up to the levels of justice required in that sphere.

Many of the sketches in this book require some sort of 'action' in the follow up. Some people will call it 'political'. The word has a very emotive quality which is used to good effect in this piece.

Characters	Garcia	An activist in a popular organization. Quick tempered, embittered and suspicious of others.
	Priest	An ordinary local priest, more used to hearing confessions than dealing with military police. Initially confused and scared, he only gradually emerges as a strong character.
	Interrogator	Intelligent, almost refined, his uniform is smart and his boots are well polished. A prisoner's death is unimportant but provides some light relief.

Stage directions

The reality of life today in many countries is reflected in the sketch. It requires great conviction to carry the two main parts. The set is small and bare, or is made to look so by screens of neutral colour forming a 'V' shape open to the audience.

Garcia is seated on a chair. He wears a loose shirt and trousers but is barefoot. He is tired and bedraggled. Keys are heard offstage and a hand pushes a priest into the cell. Garcia backs off instinctively.

PRIEST: Garcia. It is Garcia isn't it? (*He steps forward offering his hand*)

GARCIA: Yes Father. (*He ignores the hand*) I suppose you've come to give me the last rites? You needn't have bothered.

PRIEST: No, you're mistaken. I'm in the same position as you. They arrested me early this morning. I wasn't even given time to shave.

GARCIA: Ah. They've arrested you. Why should they do that?

PRIEST: Since when do they give a reason?

GARCIA: True. Sit down. I'm sorry I can't offer you anything more comfortable but the room they've given me is rather primitive.

(*The PRIEST sits. A pause.*)

PRIEST: Are you all right?

GARCIA: I'm alive.

PRIEST: What do they . . . How do they treat you?

GARCIA: It depends what mood they're in. Sometimes they give me a cigarette and chat to me about my friends in the Liberation to see if I let any names slip. Other times they kick me round the room like a football. From one to the other. They want me to sign a confession, they've drawn one up for me to save time.

PRIEST: And if you sign it?

GARCIA: (*Shrugs*) They make promises.

PRIEST: Like setting you free?

GARCIA: (*Laughs*) You're more naive than I thought, Father. Do you really think it makes any difference what I admit to? I am one of the vanished ones now. We disappear during the night. In the morning our bed is empty. Nobody asks any questions, nobody tries to look for us. Our names have been erased from public records. We never existed. You and I. (*Pause*) Do you really think they brought you here just to question you?

(*Footsteps. Keys jangle offstage. GARCIA and the PRIEST both look in the direction of the door at stage left.*)

INTERROGATOR: (*From offstage*) The Priest.

(*The PRIEST looks at GARCIA, crosses himself hurriedly and exits through the door. The keys jangle as the door is locked. After a pause GARCIA turns the chair round so that its back is to the audience. He stands behind it with both hands on the back as if he is standing in the dock. The following is spoken as if he is making his defence to the audience.*)

GARCIA: My name is Luis Garcia. I am accused of terrorist activities and membership of an illegal organization. I am guilty on both charges, I don't mind telling you. I come from a notorious family. My father was one of those dangerous subversives who kept books in the house. Not only that, he read them and taught his children what he learned.

One day I returned home to the farm to fetch some seed. There was a grey van outside the house I had never seen before. A man in uniform was carrying my father's books from his room and throwing them into the back of the van. I asked him what he was doing but he ignored me, so I ran inside. My father was in the kitchen with another of the soldiers. My sister was there too and she was crying and holding on to my father. He said that he had to go away for a while and I was to look after the family while he was gone.

Then the other soldier came back and said he wanted to take my sister outside to question her. My father became angry and started to shout but they hit him with the butt of a rifle. One of the soldiers kept us in the kitchen while the other dragged my sister outside to 'question' her. When she came back she wouldn't look at me.

They took my father away in the grey van and I never saw him again. Later I met other people who had suffered similar experiences. They had the same anger gnawing inside them as me. They told me the government called them terrorists.

(*The keys jangle again. The* PRIEST *is pushed back into the room so that he falls on his face.* GARCIA *picks him up and sits him on the chair. He breathes heavily. He has obviously been beaten.*)

GARCIA: So they play football with priests too eh?

(*The* PRIEST *smiles weakly and tries to get his breath back.*)

PRIEST: Apparently.
GARCIA: Are you all right?
PRIEST: I'm alive (*It is* GARCIA*'s turn to smile*) They seem to think I'm in league with the Liberation. They said I procure arms for you and use Church funds to finance terrorist activities.
GARCIA: Ha! If only it were true.

PRIEST: Even my sermons incite my congregation to enlist in illegal organizations that are anti-government. Have you ever heard me preach?

GARCIA: Once. It was all about our Saviour being the Lamb of God. 'Blessed are the peacemakers' you kept saying and urged us to be meek and mild like lambs being led to the slaughter.

PRIEST: There you are.

(*Pause*)

GARCIA: Don't you ever get angry? When two of them hold you and the other punches you in the belly 'til you can't stand up. Don't you want to land a fist on one of their smug smiling faces?

PRIEST: Yes I do. I'm afraid I kicked one of the guards rather hard as I went down.

GARCIA: Good, Father.

PRIEST: But I pray God will forgive me.

GARCIA: Forgive, forgive! Why does the Church have this obsession with forgiving? Can't you do something in the name of justice and believe it was right?

PRIEST: Yes, if it is in the name of justice. Isn't it more often in the name of hatred?

GARCIA: For me, Father, the two are the same thing. They took away my family, they took away my home, my land, my dignity, my right to speak. They've put me in a cell and tortured me for three months. Haven't I got the right to a little hatred? When was anything ever achieved without men becoming angry with the cruelty of others.

PRIEST: God is angry too. The Church . . .

GARCIA: The Church? What does the Church ever do? It issues statements and declarations. It raises its hands in horror at the atrocities committed in the name of national security. And then it drains off men's anger into a weak spineless thing called forgiveness. And what is actually done? Nothing. Nothing beyond a few more prayers for peace being offered up.

(*The* PRIEST *gets up and indicates the chair.*)

PRIEST: Let me stand for a while.

(*GARCIA glares at him. He resumes his seat with a sigh.*)

GARCIA: If the Church had given the Liberation army its full backing from the beginning we would be strong enough to resist the government. We don't ask you priests to carry guns, all we wanted was your support. Why couldn't you give it when it was needed?

(*A pause*)

PRIEST: Did you know Diaz?

GARCIA: Of course I know him. He's a government informer. It's common knowledge.

PRIEST: He's dead now. His house burnt down about a month ago. He was in bed asleep when it happened.

GARCIA: He should have been more careful.

PRIEST: He wasn't the first collaborator to die accidentally.

GARCIA: These people are traitors Father. Vipers who will bite the hands of their own brothers and sisters if it means there will be a little more food on their plate in the evening.

PRIEST: Does that make murder legitimate?

GARCIA: You expect us to stand by and watch the authorities buy out people with their bribes?

PRIEST: You didn't answer my question

GARCIA: (*Exasperated*) There are thousands of bodies in unmarked graves dug by the security forces . . .

PRIEST: So you must murder too?

GARCIA: If necessary, yes. In the name of justice.

PRIEST: That is your decision, before God. But don't ask me to make the Church a party to murder.

(*GARCIA spits on the ground.*)

GARCIA: No, you keep your hands clean Father. Let the Church keep its reputation and leave the fighting to godless men like me, who care more about their country than their souls.

(*The PRIEST gets up and moves over to GARCIA.*)

PRIEST: Who runs the schools here? Teaches our children? Opens hospitals, feeds the poor?

GARCIA: You do, I don't deny it. But you won't change the future of our country by putting plasters on cuts, Father. The people are being trampled on. Someone has to stand up and say 'enough'!

PRIEST: We have said that. Time and time again we have protested to the authorities.

GARCIA: Protested! It's all talk. That gets us nowhere. The time for talk is long past.

PRIEST: And has the time come for us to burn men alive while they sleep in their beds?

(*A pause. GARCIA sits on the chair.*)

GARCIA: Father, if a soldier was raping your sister, wouldn't you use a gun if it was close to hand?

PRIEST: That's an old question, Garcia, and a trick one too. I don't have to be a pacifist to oppose violence. If someone attacks my brother or sister the Lord allows me to defend them, but not by committing a greater evil than the first one. Murder is not the solution to murder.

(*GARCIA stands up unexpectedly and slaps the PRIEST on one cheek. A pause. The two men stare at each other face to face.*)

GARCIA: You want to hit me don't you Father?

(*The PRIEST turns the other cheek slowly and deliberately.*)

GARCIA: Weakness.

PRIEST: A moral victory.

GARCIA: What's the good of moral victories? They don't bring down governments.

(*Footsteps. A jangle of keys. They both look at the door.*)

INTERROGATOR: (*From offstage*) Let's have you Garcia.

(*GARCIA exits. The PRIEST sits down. Crosses himself. Puts his head in his hands and prays. After a short while he sits back and opens his eyes. The following is spoken as if he is having a dialogue out loud with God.*)

PRIEST: Yes, I am proud. How hard it is to be a priest and not be proud. I think I am better than him. He is young, headstrong, eaten up by hate. (*Pause*) Yet there is no pride in him. When I looked into his eyes they said 'What do you know about dying?' (*He looks around the cell*) This isn't what I'd expected. When I was going through seminary I remember being taught about the martyrs of the Church. I used to imagine them somehow always bathed in golden light. Tied to the stake or kneeling at an execution block saying their last prayer as the people watched and were moved by their dignity and courage. Thank you for sparing me the applause of the crowd. (*He smiles ironically*) At least he is dying for what he believes in. I am dying . . . why? Because someone in the village was hungry and decided to tell the authorities some lies about the local priest. What is there to be proud of in that sort of death? I am a poor joke, not a martyr.

(*Standing up, he paces the room in frustration.*)

PRIEST: It all seems so pointless. Who will look after my little church if I don't return? They are scared, Lord. The government on one side, the Liberation on the other, caught between the devil and the deep blue sea. They look to me for guidance, they need me. (*Pause*) Perhaps if I co-operate, give them the answers they want to hear, they'll let me go. They've got no real evidence against me. (*Angry with himself*) Listen to me! All I want is to save my own skin. A shepherd of the sheep! It's the blind leading the blind. I'm a joke!

(*The keys jangle again.* GARCIA *is pushed back into the room.*)

PRIEST: Garcia! What's happening? Did they hurt you?

(GARCIA *shakes his head for the* PRIEST *to keep quiet. He indicates the doorway by another motion of his head. The* PRIEST *realizes there is someone listening.*)

PRIEST: I hope you answered their questions truthfully. Since we are both innocent our best course of action must be to co-operate with the authorities fully.

(*The* INTERROGATOR *enters. He is wearing military uniform and has a gun in a shoulder holster.*)

INTERROGATOR: Please don't play charades for my benefit.

(*He sits in the chair. A pause while he looks at them.*)

INTERROGATOR: The priest and the terrorist, strange bed-fellows for a cell aren't you?

GARCIA: We didn't ask to be put together.

INTERROGATOR: I'm afraid we have a problem with overcrowding at the moment. Every available cell is in use. Some are used by four or five prisoners, most uncomfortable. You two are special cases.

PRIEST: Why special?

INTERROGATOR: There are grades of criminal activity. Let's say you come near the other end of the scale from someone who has been stealing sheep.

PRIEST: I still haven't been told for what crime I've been arrested.

INTERROGATOR: (*Shrugs*) It's unnecessary to be specific.

GARCIA: In other words you don't have to give reasons for torturing people.

INTERROGATOR: (*Ignoring Garcia and giving his attention to the Priest*) Your friend has been very uncooperative during his stay.

PRIEST: You have repeatedly beaten him.

INTERROGATOR: He is a terrorist. (*He takes the gun and polishes it with a cloth*) I consider we have been very patient with him. You, however, are a priest so we expect the truth without having to beat it out of you.

PRIEST: I have told you the truth.

INTERROGATOR: You have not given the information we require. Your village has become a focus for subversive activity. There are people known to both of you who are working with illegal terrorist organizations. One of you will give me the names.

(*A silence*)

INTERROGATOR: We cannot let you go on using the space in this cell forever.

(*Another pause. The silence is allowed to go on until it is unbearable.*)

PRIEST: If you're going to kill us then you might as well say so now.

INTERROGATOR: Why? Are you afraid? I thought a priest's soul flies straight to heaven when he dies. (*He puts the gun to the Priest's temple*) I would be doing you a favour wouldn't I? Or perhaps you have doubts. Perhaps there are things God knows about you that will damn your soul. All men have secrets. What about the terrorist? (*He crosses to Garcia and puts the gun to his head*) Is he secretly a Christian? Will God overlook murder and arson because it was done in the name of freedom? (*Mimicking God*) 'Ah, yes, this was the one who blew some soldiers to pieces with a petrol bomb, but at least he was sincere.' What is worth more, the life of a terrorist or the life of a priest? (*He takes the gun away*)

An interesting question when you put it like that. But who am I, a mere soldier, to judge in such an issue? (*He sits in the chair again*) No one but the Almighty can decide, isn't that so Father? And yet who can know the mind of God? If I shoot the terrorist through the head now, is it an act of providence or am I committing a sin?

GARCIA: Is this some kind of game?

INTERROGATOR: (*Considers*) For me, yes. For you it is very serious. My superiors are impatient, they say we are wasting too much time on troublemakers. Regrettably I have to kill one of you.

PRIEST: One of us?

INTERROGATOR: I have persuaded them that you may still possess valuable information.

PRIEST: Neither of us will tell you anything.

INTERROGATOR: Perhaps. Perhaps I will eventually release one of you, but at the moment I'm more concerned with who to kill. (*Pause*) Why don't I let you decide? (*He sits back in the chair, enjoying the effect of his suggestion*)

GARCIA: We decide which one of us lives?

INTERROGATOR: Exactly.

GARCIA: Don't be absurd! Neither of us are going to volunteer to die.

INTERROGATOR: It's up to you. If you can't decide I'll shoot whoever I please. (*He looks at his watch*) I'll give you one minute.

(*GARCIA and the PRIEST look at each other. They move downstage and talk in fast whispers.*)

GARCIA: He's enjoying this. Playing God.

PRIEST: Let me die.

GARCIA: No. You're not going to cheat me.

PRIEST: Cheat you?

GARCIA: Of dying for the Liberation. I've waited for this.

PRIEST: You're younger than me.

GARCIA: What does that matter? You don't care about the Liberation.

PRIEST: That isn't what you'd be dying for.

GARCIA: What else?

PRIEST: For me. He's giving us a straight choice, one of us can live. If you die, it's to give me that chance.

GARCIA: (*Bewildered*) You?

PRIEST: Yes. Think about it. Do you want to die to save a priest's life?

GARCIA: But ... I don't understand ... why should you die any more than me? To save a terrorist?

PRIEST: To save a brother. That is the calling of my faith. Yours is only to die for your cause.

GARCIA: I ...

INTERROGATOR: (*Standing up*) One minute is up. Who's ready to die, the priest or the terrorist?

(*He raises the gun to point it at them. All three hold a freeze. Blackout.*)

Bible notes

Created social The creation stories show that the social dimension of human beings is as much a part of their essential humanity as the physical, mental and spiritual aspects of their life. Made in God's image, made male and female, made to multiply, people need people in both the bonds of family and wider social relationships.

Divided society and God's mission The stories of Genesis 3-11, in particular the Tower of Babel and the Flood, show these relationships breaking down as society was increasingly characterized by violence and division. But God's answer to this situation is the call of Abraham, and the promise of a new kind of society through which all nations on earth would be blessed. This redemptive purpose of God for humanity is a basis for all Christian mission. It is achieved not merely in individuals but is also closely linked to a new social order among the people of God. The people of God had to 'do righteousness and justice' (Genesis 18:19) for God to fulfil his promise to Abraham. The social and political spheres are closely bound to the spiritual sphere.

It is sometimes said that Jesus had no interest in politics and preached a purely individual, spiritual message. But we should remember that:

1 Jesus endorsed the total message of the Old Testament.
2 Jesus was perceived as a political threat and crucified as such, so his message, if not political in a campaigning sense, was radically disturbing to the interests of the political status quo.
3 His life shows he saw his mission in holistic terms — i.e. meeting the whole needs of whole people in their whole social context. Jesus brought evangelism and social action together; not only was his physical care for people a means for them to enter the Kingdom of God but also profound changes in lifestyle often occurred when people accepted him.
4 There is much evidence that Jesus was deeply concerned about the politics of his times and shared the aspirations to freedom of many people of the time (aspirations shown in the early songs and stories in Luke — Luke 1:46-55 and 4:16-20), though he was critical of the methods advocated by groups like the Zealots.

Follow up

Questions

1 What do you think of Garcia and his stand as a terrorist?
   Does it relate to any experience of your own?

2 What would be your definitions of 'social action for justice', and
   'political action'?

3 To what extent are you prepared to work for social justice, and where
   would you draw the line at 'being involved'?

Things to do

- Make a scrap book or display about news items concerning people who
  are suffering for their beliefs or in the struggle for justice.

- Amnesty International have a scheme for groups who want to work for
  a fair hearing for political prisoners. Contact them and find out how
  you can help. (Address on page 124.)

- Find out what are the social issues that matter most to the people who
  live in your area. Examine the local church's attitude and response to
  these issues.

The Great Tractor Race

by Andrew Goreing

In the Old Testament, God sought to create a society in which help for the poor and needy was more than just charity hand-outs. It was based on a fair distribution of the economic resources of the nation. Long term features to promote equal opportunities were built into the organization of society. However, international trade pays no attention to God's moral principles. In this sketch the attitude and power of wealthy nations are exposed in a humorous style but with tragic consequences. This is a challenging script, but the time and effort needed for its production will be well worthwhile. Careful direction is essential, especially of the extensive use of props.

Characters   Narrator
              Charlie One
              Charlie Two
              Thompson One
              Thompson Two

Stage directions
One side of the acting area will represent the land of the Thompsons, which will have a desk and chairs and maybe some other office paraphernalia such as a hat stand. The other side is the home of the Charlies. Props required include bowler hats, umbrellas, fake microphone, some carrots, tray of glasses, soda fountain, two toy tractors, jelly babies, seed packets, a bag marked 'Emergency Food Aid' full of something like semi-pulverized peanuts, toy money, two plates, salt, pepper, cutlery, flower pots or similar, watering can.

(*The first part of the sketch ignores the division of the stage. We begin with just the* NARRATOR *on stage.*)

NARRATOR: We have but one world. One world to live in. One world to share. We look at the sparkling prodigality of the night sky — world upon world, heaven within heaven — and we reflect; this earth is all we have. Yet, however far our imaginations rove, through however many galaxies the eye of humanity gazes, in every corner of the universe we find one eternal law, one law acknowledged by every being — by creatures angelic, human, animal, hydro-electric, acknowledged by life-forms to us quite unimaginable. (*Pause*) In every pantomime horse . . . somebody has to be the back legs. Or, as they say on the quasi-silica-zirconite satellites of Betelgeuz — 'There's always a Charlie.' (*Calls*) Charlie!

(*Two CHARLIES dash onstage.*)

NARRATOR: And sometimes two. I want two volunteers.

(*CHARLIES stick up their hands, 'Me!' 'Please!' etc.*)

NARRATOR: Thank you — to represent the poor nations of the world, the wretched of the earth. And two volunteers —

(*The THOMPSONS appear; smart, each with bowler hat and umbrella.*)

NARRATOR: To represent the rich.

THOMPSONS: (*In unison*) How do you do? Thompson's the name . . . Funny . . . (*As they realize they are talking in chorus*)

NARRATOR: Sometimes the relationship between the rich and the poor is very clear.

THOMPSON ONE: How d'you do. Thompson's the name.

CHARLIE ONE: Charlie. Very pleased to m-

THOMPSON ONE: Tut tut tut.

CHARLIE ONE: Sorry?

THOMPSON ONE: You don't look too good.

NARRATOR: It consists of compassion.

THOMPSON ONE: Here's a few bob to see you through till Christmas.

CHARLIE ONE: Oh. Thanks.

NARRATOR: Concern.

THOMPSON ONE: Let's have a look at you.

(*THOMPSON ONE inspects CHARLIE ONE, peering inside his mouth, tugging at his ears, poking at his tummy, checking if his hands are clean, etc, etc.*)

THOMPSON ONE: Dear dear. You're not in very good shape at all, are you? Not at all. In fact, you've got a surfeit. You're suffering from an all round surfeit of shortage. Tut tut.

NARRATOR: Advice.

THOMPSON ONE: Hard work! That's the answer!

CHARLIE ONE: Hard work? How hard?

THOMPSON ONE: Get down to it!

(*CHARLIE ONE promptly crouches.*)

THOMPSON ONE: . . . Lower! A bit more.

NARRATOR: And partnership.

(*THOMPSON ONE sits astride CHARLIE ONE's shoulders.*)

THOMPSON ONE: Giddee-up!

(*CHARLIE ONE stands, lifting THOMPSON ONE aloft. THOMPSON ONE produces a carrot and dangles it just out of CHARLIE ONE's reach.*

THOMPSON TWO watches this scene, and promptly bashes CHARLIE TWO with his umbrella. CHARLIE TWO wilts and THOMPSON TWO also climbs into the saddle.)

NARRATOR: With various degrees of coercion.

(*Another bash from THOMPSON TWO's umbrella and CHARLIE TWO stands.*)

NARRATOR: And various degrees of reward.

(*THOMPSON TWO produces a tiny carrot.*)

NARRATOR: (*Shrugs*) But that's the way of the world. (*He produces a microphone and proffers it to THOMPSON ONE*)

THOMPSON ONE: Enterprize, dedication, hard work, micro-computers, division of labour, the invisible hand of the market, opportunities for all in the brave new world of the sunrise industries, let us go forward together into the twenty-first century, a new day is dawning, peace, prosperity and security, humanity comes of age in the kingdom of freedom.

(*Microphone switched to CHARLIE ONE.*)

CHARLIE ONE: (*Pause*) Backache.

(*Microphone switched back to THOMPSON ONE.*)

THOMPSON ONE: Best endeavours, rectify anomalies, plain to see those less fortunate, moral obligations laid on all who, unhappy situation of, through no fault of those who, extend the helping hand whenever possible, write on both sides of the paper, use block capitals, delete where applicable.

CHARLIE ONE: (*Pause*) Bellyache.

THOMPSON ONE: Unfortunately, revision of aid budgets, essential belts tighten, recession biting deeper than expected.

(*THOMPSON ONE takes a big bite out of the carrot.*
THOMPSON TWO scoffs his carrot and bashes CHARLIE TWO with the umbrella for good measure.)

NARRATOR: Perhaps you think we are overstating the case. The position is rarely so obvious.

(*The THOMPSONS dismount. The CHARLIES lean on each other to rest.*)

NARRATOR: Sometimes the cords that connect rich and poor are elusive. Invisible. But the actions of the rich still reap their harvest among the poor. (*He produces a tray of drinks for the THOMPSONS.*) Drink, sir?

THOMPSON ONE: (*Offering a glass to THOMPSON TWO*) It's an unsophisticated little petroleum, but I think you'll find its *ingenue* naivety quite tantalizing.

THOMPSON TWO: Hmm. A fruity, full-bodied oil. What do you think?

THOMPSON ONE: (*Tasting*) Crude. Wouldn't give more than fourteen dollars a barrel. Try some of this.

THOMPSON TWO: What is it?

THOMPSON ONE: Tea.

CHARLIE TWO: Don't drink!

THOMPSON TWO: I'm sorry?

CHARLIE ONE: Don't touch it! It's poison!

THOMPSON ONE: It looks perfectly all right to me. Your health.

CHARLIE TWO: Please! It's poison, I assure you.

THOMPSON TWO: Nonsense. (*Drinks*) Very refreshing.

(*Pause. CHARLIE TWO groans and doubles up. The THOMPSONS look at him quizzically, then at the drink. THOMPSON TWO takes another sip and CHARLIE TWO becomes iller. The THOMPSONS return to the other drinks, guzzling them enthusiastically.*)

THOMPSON ONE: Here. Bauxite.
THOMPSON TWO: Cheers. Manganese nodules.
THOMPSON ONE: Mmm! Polyvinylchloride.
THOMPSON TWO: Aluminium.
THOMPSON ONE: Cotton.
THOMPSON TWO: Coffee.
THOMPSON ONE: Silver.
THOMPSON TWO: Uranium.

(*Both* CHARLIES *deteriorate with each drink until they are lying on the floor, croaking feebly.*)

CHARLIE ONE: Water . . . water . . .
THOMPSON ONE: Good idea. Water?
THOMPSON TWO: Thanks.

(THOMPSON ONE *takes the soda fountain from the drinks tray and pours a squirt for himself and* THOMPSON TWO.)

CHARLIES: Water . . .

(*The* THOMPSONS *look at each other, then at the* CHARLIES, *then at the soda, then . . .*)

NARRATOR: (*Intervenes, shaking his finger*) Now, now. (*Remove drinks etc.*) Perhaps those connections were a little too elusive. To make things a bit clearer, we present 'World Trade in a Nutshell' —

(*Crunch! The* THOMPSONS *are miming eating walnuts — or doing so for real.*)

NARRATOR: 'World Trade in a Nutshell', also known as 'The Great Tractor Race'.

(THOMPSONS *and* CHARLIES *begin to move to their respective sides of the world.*)

NARRATOR: Come with me, if you will, halfway across the world, on a trip to the tropics —
THOMPSONS: (*In unison*) My God, Daphne, the heat. (*Each slaps his neck to kill a mosquito*)
NARRATOR: To the land of the CHARLIES. Here in this banana para-

dise, where the sun beats down twenty four hours a day —

THOMPSONS: (*In unison*) My God, Daphne, the heat. (*Slap*)

NARRATOR: The people scratch a meagre living from the sun-baked soil, relying on their staple crop of — ?

CHARLIE ONE: (*Pause*) Carrots.

NARRATOR: Carrots?

CHARLIE ONE: Carrots.

NARRATOR: Their staple crop of . . . carrots. In a good year, there are enough carrots for everyone. In a bad year, there are some who go hungry. But although life is hard, and work on the . . . carrot plantations is heavy, the people are happy.

CHARLIE TWO: And our eyesight is amazing.

NARRATOR: (*Producing seed trays or flowerpots*) The carrot plantations. The mighty . . . carrot palms, wafting their fronds in the breeze . . . the tropical sun —

THOMPSONS AND CHARLIES: (*In unison*) My God, Daphne, the heat. (*Slap*)

NARRATOR: A timeless scene. Until —

CHARLIE ONE: Charlie?

CHARLIE TWO: Yes, Charlie?

NARRATOR: Progress strikes.

CHARLIE ONE: I've been thinking.

CHARLIE TWO: Have a lie down, then.

CHARLIE ONE: No, listen. I'm thinking carrots.

CHARLIE TWO: Surprise me.

CHARLIE ONE: I'm thinking, if we doubled our annual carrot yield, we'd be twice as well off.

CHARLIE TWO: Charlie Einstein, that's what they call him.

CHARLIE ONE: And if we produced more carrots with less work, we could use our spare time to diversify!

CHARLIE TWO: Swedes as well, you mean?

CHARLIE ONE: Yes!

CHARLIE TWO: Don't like Swedes.

CHARLIE ONE: Nonsense. You've never tried them.

CHARLIE TWO: I've heard Abba. Don't like Swedes and I'm sick of carrots.

CHARLIE ONE: We need a tractor. If we had a tractor, the cultivation of the carrot fields would only take half the time. And we wouldn't have to go ploughing with that lousy ox.

CHARLIE TWO: True.

CHARLIE ONE: We could eat the ox.

CHARLIE TWO: That's a bit rough, after a lifetime's service.

CHARLIE ONE: You can't stop progress. We'll get a tractor, then. Agreed?

CHARLIE TWO: Agreed. Where do we get one?

CHARLIE ONE: From the Thompsons!

(*CHARLIE ONE goes over to the* THOMPSONS, *now seated behind their desk.*)

CHARLIE ONE: I'd like a tractor please!

THOMPSON ONE: Can you pay?

CHARLIE ONE: No.

THOMPSON ONE: Next door.

CHARLIE ONE: Next door?

THOMPSON ONE: Office of Foreign Trade and Overseas Development.

THOMPSON TWO: Can I help you?

CHARLIE ONE: I'd like a tractor please.

THOMPSON TWO: Can you pay?

CHARLIE ONE: No.

THOMPSON TWO: What are you growing?

CHARLIE ONE: Carrots.

THOMPSON TWO: That's no good. We've got plenty of carrots.

CHARLIE ONE: That's all we've got.

THOMPSON TWO: All right. Here's the plan.

(*During this speech* THOMPSON TWO *produces, when appropriate, money, toy tractors, carrots and jellybabies, and whizzes them around the desk in illustration.*)

THOMPSON TWO: We lend you the money to buy a tractor. You pay us, we deliver the tractor, you pay us back, plus interest, out of your foreign exchange. Dig up half your carrots (*carrot flung off stage*) and plant jellybabies. We like jellybabies. (*Munch*) You can have one tractor cheap for the jellybaby fields, and one full price for the carrot fields, sell us the jellybabies, we pay you, you pay us back the money we paid you to pay for the tractor. Got that?

CHARLIE ONE: Er.

THOMPSON TWO: It's quite simple. Jellybaby production booms, carrot production booms. (*Carrots and jellybabies flung into the air*) Money pours in. Buy more tractors. More production, more jellybabies, more diversification of the economy, contribution to world trade, and everything's coming up carrots. Industrialization, urbanization, social security, early retirement, higher education, you join the front rank of the world's trading nations and become one of the super-powers of the twenty-first century. (*Pause*) Amazing things, tractors.

CHARLIE ONE: It's a deal!

(*Now things speed up. CHARLIE ONE dashes home, upturns a seed tray, flinging carrots off stage.*)

CHARLIE ONE: We're planting jellybabies!

(*CHARLIE ONE dashes back to the desk and grabs a tractor and a packet of seeds. He sets off home. Halfway home the THOMPSONS whistle for him and he returns to the desk. The THOMPSONS take back the tractor and give CHARLIE ONE cash. They then take back half the cash and return the tractor. CHARLIE ONE dashes home, forgetting the seed packet.*)

CHARLIE TWO: Planting what?

CHARLIE ONE: Jellybabies. Jellybabies! Aagh!

(*CHARLIE ONE scuttles back for the seeds, grabs them and another tractor. He is halfway home when the THOMPSONS whistle. He returns, puts down more cash and is given a watering can. He returns home, forgetting the tractors.*)

CHARLIE ONE: Plant the seeds. Need water.

CHARLIE TWO: That's never a tractor.

CHARLIE ONE: The tractor! (*Zooms back to the desk, puts down more cash, takes the tractors, home again*) Tractors!

CHARLIE TWO: (*Tipping the can*) No water.

CHARLIE ONE: No water! (*Grabs can, back to the desk*) No water.

(*The THOMPSONS squirt soda into the can. CHARLIE ONE dashes home but the THOMPSONS whistle and he returns, pays over his last note and goes home again. The* CHARLIES *water the jellybaby seeds.*)

THOMPSONS: Jellybabies! Jellybabies! Jellybabies! (*Singing*) Why
    are we waiting, why are we waiting, why oh why —
CHARLIE ONE: Yes!

(*Jellybabies harvested.* CHARLIE ONE *grabs a handful, runs and
delivers them to the* THOMPSONS' *desk.* THOMPSON TWO *starts tossing
them idly, one by one, into* THOMPSON ONE'S *mouth.* CHARLIE ONE *goes
home but* THOMPSON TWO *whistles and* CHARLIE ONE *returns. He is
given money and goes home.*)

CHARLIE ONE: Money!
CHARLIE TWO: Carrots.
CHARLIE ONE: Carrots?
CHARLIE TWO: We've eaten all the carrots.
CHARLIE ONE: What?
CHARLIE TWO: Carrot famine.
CHARLIE ONE: No carrots?
CHARLIE TWO: No.
CHARLIE ONE: Oh no.
CHARLIE TWO: Eat the jellybabies!
CHARLIE ONE: No! Get off! Don't touch! I'll buy some carrots.
CHARLIE TWO: Carrots . . .

(CHARLIE ONE *dashes back to the* THOMPSONS.)

CHARLIE ONE: Carrots!
THOMPSON TWO: Carrots?
CHARLIE ONE: Yes.

(THOMPSON TWO *hands over his umbrella.* CHARLIE ONE *dashes home —
halfway there he stops and looks at the umbrella.*)

CHARLIE ONE: Carrots?
THOMPSON TWO: Umbrella.
CHARLIE ONE: Oh.
CHARLIE TWO: (*About to eat the rest of the jellybaby harvest*)
    Jellybabies!
CHARLIE ONE: No! (*Dashes home and bashes* CHARLIE TWO *with the
    umbrella*)

CHARLIE TWO: Ooogh. (*Rolls over*)

(*There is a whistle from the* THOMPSONS *and* CHARLIE ONE *returns to the desk, taking the jellybabies. He is paid. He then puts half the money back on the table and is given some carrots. He returns home and shoves a carrot into the mouth of the recovering* CHARLIE TWO. CHARLIE ONE *then comes to a panting halt and reviews the situation.*)

CHARLIE ONE: Carrots, tractor, jellybabies, umbrella, carrots, tractor, jellybabies, umbrella, carrots, tractor — another tractor, another tractor, more carrots.

CHARLIE TWO: (*Sitting up*) No more tractors! Jellybabies!

(CHARLIE ONE *bashes him with umbrella; further collapse of* CHARLIE TWO.)

CHARLIE ONE: Jellybabies.

THOMPSON TWO: (*Calling for more*) Jellybabies!

(CHARLIE ONE *ferries more jellybabies to the* THOMPSONS *and then goes home again.*)

CHARLIE ONE: Carrots, tractor, jellybabies, umbrella, carrots, tractor, jellybabies, umbrella.

CHARLIE TWO: (*Feebly*) Carrots . . . carrots . . .

CHARLIE ONE: Carrots?

THOMPSON TWO: Jellybabies!

(CHARLIE ONE *dashes to the desk with more jellybabies. He is paid. Halfway home he stops and looks at the money — it's just one note or coin. He stares at it in alarm and looks back at* THOMPSON TWO.)

THOMPSON TWO: I'm terribly sorry. I'm afraid the world market price of jellybabies has gone through the floor. There's a glut, you see.

(THOMPSON ONE, *who has been having his mouth stuffed with jellybabies for the last minute or so, splurts them all out. Jellybabies spray across the stage.*

CHARLIE ONE *dashes home.*)

CHARLIE TWO: . . . Carrots . . .

(*CHARLIE ONE runs back to the desk.*)

CHARLIE ONE: Carrots!
THOMPSON TWO: I'm afraid there's a world shortage of carrots. The price has gone through the roof.

(*CHARLIE ONE returns home and stuffs the last of his money into CHARLIE TWO'S mouth. TWO spits it out and looks at it. He is about to take a bite when . . .*)

THOMPSON TWO: (*Whistle*) Interest repayments due!

(*CHARLIE ONE snatches the money, dashes to the desk, flings the money down, zooms home.*)

CHARLIE TWO: Carrots?
CHARLIE ONE: No.
CHARLIE TWO: Jellybabies?
CHARLIE ONE: No.
CHARLIE TWO: Money?
CHARLIE ONE: No.

(*Pause. CHARLIE TWO produces two plates with cutlery, salt and pepper, puts a tractor on each plate and offers one to CHARLIE ONE.*)

CHARLIE ONE: (*To the THOMPSONS*) We can't eat tractors!
THOMPSON TWO: Certainly not. (*To THOMPSON ONE*) Repossess the tractors!
THOMPSON ONE: This is a case of genuine need.
THOMPSON TWO: Granted.
THOMPSONS: (*In unison*) We have a moral duty to assist.
THOMPSON TWO: Jellybaby?
THOMPSON ONE: Thank you.
THOMPSONS: (*In unison*) Emergency aid is called for.
THOMPSON TWO: If you'd be so kind, Thompson.
THOMPSON ONE: Certainly, Thompson.

(*THOMPSON ONE takes a chair and a bag of emergency food aid over to the CHARLIES. He gets on the chair and holds the bag aloft.*)

CHARLIE TWO: What's he doing up there?
THOMPSON TWO: This is the trickle-down theory.

(*THOMPSON ONE snips off the corner of the bag and starts to pour a thin stream of food down onto the* CHARLIES. *They try to catch it on their plates.*)

THOMPSON TWO: Now of course, this is not a very efficient way of combatting hunger.
THOMPSON ONE: Absolutely not.

(*As* THOMPSON ONE *replies he tends to gesture with his arms, thereby sending the food stream off in various directions, the* CHARLIES *scrambling after it.*)

THOMPSON TWO: It creates dependency.
THOMPSON ONE: I'm afraid it does.
THOMPSON TWO: And corrupt administrations divert valuable resources into their own pockets.
THOMPSON ONE: Indisputably the case.
THOMPSON TWO: It's so much better to provide the poorest nations with the wherewithal to feed themselves.
THOMPSON ONE: Much.
THOMPSON TWO: To provide the know-how, the skills, the infrastructure, and then to let the locals take over and nurture the seeds of their own development. (*Pause*) Perhaps they'd be interested in some tractors.

(*The now empty food aid bag is thrown aside.* THOMPSON ONE *goes home. The* NARRATOR *returns, bringing drinks for the* THOMPSONS. NARRATOR *then moves upstage centre, holding a book.*)

THOMPSON TWO: So how did you find the Third World?
THOMPSON ONE: Terrible, Thompson, terrible. We have no idea of the poverty involved.
THOMPSON TWO: I'm sure we don't, Thompson. Cheers.
THOMPSON ONE: Cheers.

(*They drink. As before, the* CHARLIES *are hit by the poison.*)

THOMPSON TWO: Of course, the corruption is phenomenal.
THOMPSON ONE: Oh yes.

(*They drink. The* CHARLIES *groan and fall.*)

THOMPSON ONE: We do our best, but it's so hard to get to the right people.

THOMPSON TWO: I know. (*Drink*)

THOMPSON TWO: We live in an unequal world.

THOMPSON ONE: Sad but true. (*Drink*)

THOMPSON ONE: It's up to us in the West to make a few sacrifices.

THOMPSON TWO: Absolutely. (*Drink*)

NARRATOR: God says — I'm not interested in your sacrifices. Hate what is evil, love what is right, see that justice prevails.

(*The* CHARLIES, *by now very weak, call 'Water . . . water . . .'.*)

THOMPSON TWO: Makes you so grateful for what you have.

THOMPSON ONE: And all the more ready to give.

THOMPSON TWO: Roll on Christian Aid Week (*or 'Family Fast Day', as appropriate*) (*Drink*)

NARRATOR: I hate your religious festivals. I cannot stand them.

THOMPSON TWO: Cheers.

THOMPSON ONE: Cheers.

(*They drink*)

NARRATOR: Let justice flow down like a stream, and righteousness like a river that never runs dry.

CHARLIES: (*Faint*) Water . . . water . . .

(*Blackout.*)

Bible notes

Multinational companies, grain mountains and overseas aid packages did not exist in Biblical times and so precise guidelines on matters of this sort are not provided. However, God's principles of fair dealing and right relationships shed light on our contemporary trading situation.

The Old Testament law was intended to create a society that was to be a model to surrounding nations. Israel was to be a country where justice was seen to be done. The structure of the economy was such that the rights of the poor were safeguarded: Hebrew slaves were freed every seventh year (Exodus 21:2) and land was returned to its original owner at the Jubilee (Leviticus 25). Such measures prevented the poor being caught in a downward spiral of poverty.

However, the prophets revealed that God's laws were not being obeyed and that unfair deals had become commonplace. Amos condemned the use of dishonest scales, skimping measures and selling the floor sweepings with the wheat (Amos 8:4-6).

Although such practices still occur in today's world, the main area of unjust trade is the relationship between rich and poor countries. The world trading system works for the benefit of the rich and powerful. Nations with essential economic resources and firms with monopolies in the commodity market are able to call the tune to the disadvantage of weaker nations. In the story of the rich man and Lazarus (Luke 16:19-31), Jesus condemns the unjust relationship between rich and poor and implies that the rich man was judged precisely because he did nothing to change the situation.

Exploitative and uncaring relationships are always condemned in the Bible, particularly when between wealthy and poor. James highlights the luxury and self-indulgence of the rich which only came at the expense of the poor (James 2:1-13) and he encourages all Christians to treat other people in the same way as they would like God to treat them.

The good news of Jesus's messianic proclamation in Luke 4:16-21 encompasses the freeing of the oppressed. Where an unjust system causes oppression and gives unfair advantages to any special group, we should work to recreate that system. Today the system of world trade must be understood like this, so that God's principles of fair dealing and right relationships are restored.

Follow up

Questions

1 Were the Charlies wrong to want to be more efficient?

2 If you had been in the position of the Thompsons what would you have done?

3 In trying to achieve justice for the Charlies, which is more valuable: giving aid, or campaigning for fairer trade and better prices for their produce?

Things to do

● Contact your local M.P. and find out about his or her party's policy on overseas aid. Is it tied to buying British goods or products?

● Review your own attitude to giving and think about the values that, as a Christian, should be important. Ask your church to do the same.

● Have you heard of Christian Aid's *Project Focus* scheme and CAFOD's *Partnership Scheme*? Join one of these schemes and find out about the type of work Christian Aid and CAFOD support and the emphasis placed on long term development. The materials provided include pictures, information sheets and project updates. (For these and other addresses, see pp. 124-5.)

Resources are available from the following development agencies and resource centres. Please remember to enclose a large, stamped addressed envelope and to contact them well in advance of when you need the material.

Development agencies

CAFOD 2 Garden Close, Stockwell Road, London SW9 9TY Tel. 01-733 7900.

CHRISTIAN AID   P.O. Box 1, London SW9 8BH Tel. 01-733 5500

SCIAF (Scottish International Aid Fund) 43 Greenhill Road, Rutherglen, Glasgow G73 2SW

TROCAIRE   169 Booterstown Avenue, Blackrock, Co. Dublin, Eire

AUSTRALIAN CATHOLIC RELIEF   154 Elizabeth Street, Sydney 2000, Australia

WORLD CHRISTIAN ACTION   Australian Council of Churches, Box C199, Sydney 2000, Australia

CANADIAN CATHOLIC ORGANIZATION FOR DEVELOPMENT AND PEACE   67 Bond Street, Room 305, Toronto, Ontario M5B 1X5, Canada

CANADIAN COUNCIL OF CHURCHES   40 St Clair Avenue East, Suite 201, Toronto, Ontario M4T 1M9, Canada

NEW ZEALAND CATHOLIC COMMISSION FOR EVANGELIZATION, JUSTICE AND DEVELOPMENT   P.O. Box 12-193, Wellington, New Zealand

CHRISTIAN WORLD SERVICE   P.O. Box 297, Christchurch, New Zealand

CATHOLIC RELIEF SERVICES   1011 First Avenue, New York, NY 10022, USA

CHURCH WORLD SERVICE   475 Riverside Drive, New York, NY 10115, USA

Resource centres

AMNESTY INTERNATIONAL   5 Roberts Place, Off Bowling Green Lane, London EC1 0EJ

ANTI-SLAVERY SOCIETY   180 Brixton Road, London SW1 6AT (Literature on all aspects of contemporary slavery)

CATHOLIC INSTITUTE FOR INTERNATIONAL RELATIONS 22 Coleman Fields, London N1 7AF

CENTRE FOR WORLD DEVELOPMENT EDUCATION 128 Buckingham Palace Road, London SW1

ONE WORLD WEEK OFFICE   P.O. Box 1, London SW9 8BH

TRAIDCRAFT   (A Christian alternative marketing organization) Team Valley Trading Estate, Kingsway, Gateshead NE11 0NE (Write for free catalogue)

WORLD DEVELOPMENT MOVEMENT Bedford Chambers, Covent Garden, London WC2E 8HA

WORLD HEALTH ORGANIZATION Avenue Appia, CH/1211 Geneva 27, Switzerland

RADIUS   (The Religious Drama Society of Great Britain), St Paul's Church, Covent Garden, Bedford Street, London WC2E 9ED (Extensive drama library)

ABCUL LTD.   (Association of British Credit Unions) P.O. Box 135, Skelmersdale, Lancashire WN8 8AP

Harrison, Paul, *Inside the Third World: an anatomy of poverty,* Harmondsworth, Penguin 1979

Stott, J. R. W., *Issues Facing Christians Today,* London, Marshall 1984

Wallis, Jim, *Call to Conversion,* London, Lion Publishing 1982

Stickley, Steve and Janet, and Belben, Jim, *Using the Bible in Drama,* London, Bible Society 1980

Burbridge, Paul and Watts, Murray, *Time to Act,* London, Hodder & Stoughton 1979

Lamont, Gordon and Ronni, *Move Yourselves,* London, Bible Society 1983

George, Susan, *How the Other Half Dies,* London, Pelican (Available from CAFOD)

Sider, Ronald, *Rich Christians in an Age of Hunger,* London, Hodder & Stoughton 1977 (Available from CAFOD and Christian Aid)

BIOGRAPHICAL NOTES
ON AUTHORS

Martin Leach and Kevin Yell are the editors of *Act Justly* and take responsibility for all the bits of the book that nobody else will own up to.

MARTIN LEACH has been Youth Education Adviser at Christian Aid since 1984, and produces resources for young people who want to understand world development from a Christian perspective. Previously he worked in agriculture in Fiji where in his spare time he was director of 'New Life Theatre', a Christian drama group.

From being a drama and R.E. teacher as well as a professional actor, KEVIN YELL joined CAFOD to plan and co-ordinate the special events for the 1987 CAFOD Silver Jubilee Year. His special interest is the use of the performing arts in liturgy and religious education.

JIM BELBEN is the editor of youth resources and drama publications for the Bible Society. An ex-dishwasher, travel courier and youth worker, Jim co-wrote *Using the Bible in Drama*. He now lives in South London and is one of the Morely playwrights.

JOHN COUTTS is a lecturer in Religious Studies at the Thames Polytechnic. Having worked as a missionary in Nigeria, he now contributes to local, national and overseas broadcasting and has written two television series. He is the author of a number of sketches, plays and prize-winning poems and has also published books on religious education and theology.

Brought up and educated in Bishop's Stortford, ANDREW GOREING is now a full time writer. He has written plays for radio and television and his play *Promise* went on tour with the Riding Lights Theatre Company in 1982. Andrew now lives with his wife Karen and his daughter Hannah in East London.

ROGER HARINGTON is an Anglican priest and the Director of Jabbok Theatre Company. He stopped being a parish priest in order to direct CATS Mill Theatre in Leeds, which is part of a special project for the unemployed.

ALAN MACDONALD is the playwright and co-director of Footprints Theatre Company. He is also a freelance writer for radio and of plays for children and adults. He now lives in the Midlands and is currently writing a new drama book with Steve Stickley.

NEAL MASON was born in Middlesex and educated in Norfolk. Before establishing a career in writing, Neal travelled extensively, working his way around Europe. He has won many prizes in writing competitions and has had much work published. Neal now lives in South Wales.

SIMON PARKE is an Anglican priest, living in West London. He is married with two children and has written for radio and television and for Christian organizations. Simon says he still finds it 'easier to write justly than to act justly!'

Founder member and co-director of Footprints Theatre Company, STEVE STICKLEY has worked in professional theatre since 1977, creating original drama for all ages. With his wife, Janet, he co-wrote *Using the Bible in Drama* and *Footnotes*. They live in Nottingham with their two children Joel and Daisy.

JO RIGARLSFORD is a housewife and mother living in Leeds. She has performed many times with Jabbok Theatre Company both live and on the radio.

HUGH STEADMAN WILLIAMS is a playwright and producer and is the Artistic Director of Westminster Productions. He has written ten theatre shows and two radio plays for the BBC. Having travelled extensively on five continents, Hugh is now an Elder in the United Reformed Church and a Moral Re-Armament worker. He lives in Surrey with his artist wife and two sons.

MARTIN WILLIAMS was a student at Leeds University when he worked on *The Tea Shop*. He then went to teach English in Italy and is now in business there.

THE REVD DR CHRIS WRIGHT provided most of the material for the Bible notes. He is a lecturer at Union Biblical Seminary in Pune, India, and his specialist subject is Old Testament Ethics. He has worked as an Anglican minister in south-east England.